BIBLICAL PRINCIPLES OF CHURCH GROWTH

BIBLICAL PRINCIPLES OF CHURCH GROWTH

by
Kenneth C. Fleming

Walterick Publishers
P.O. Box 2216
Kansas City, KS 66110-0216

ISBN 0-937396-95-8

©1993 Walterick Publishers, Inc.

Table of Contents

INTRODUCTION -- THE BIBLICAL DATA BASE 9

CHAPTER 1 -- THE CHURCH IN ANTIOCH 13
"Considerable numbers were brought to the Lord" (Acts 11:21)

CHAPTER 2 -- THE CHURCHES IN GALATIA 29
"The churches were being strengthened and increasing in number daily" (Acts 16:5)

CHAPTER 3 -- THE CHURCH IN PHILIPPI 49
"I thank my God....in view of your participation in the Gospel" (Phil. 1:3-5)

CHAPTER 4 -- THE CHURCH IN THESSALONICA 67
"You became an example to all the believers in Macedonia and Achaia" (1 Thess. 1:7)

CHAPTER 5 -- THE CHURCH IN CORINTH 83
"I planted, Apollos watered, but God was causing the growth" (1 Cor. 3:6)

CHAPTER 6 -- THE CHURCH IN EPHESUS 99
"The word of the Lord was growing mightily and prevailing" (Acts 19:20)

CHAPTER 7 -- CONCLUSION 121

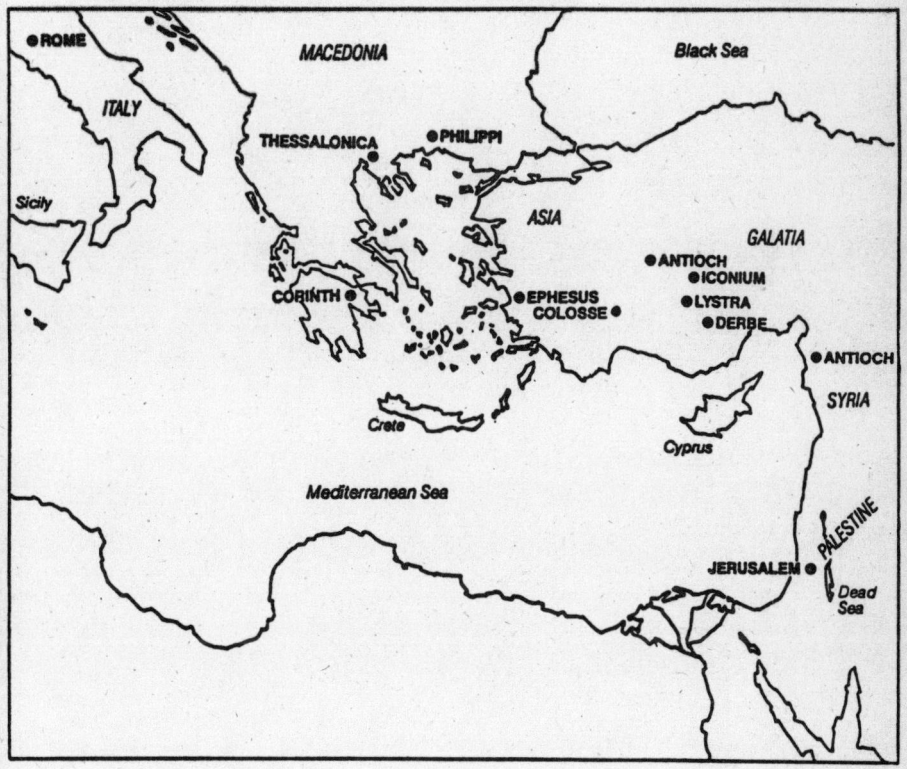

INTRODUCTION

The first century was the harbinger of the Christian era. A Man called Jesus rose from the dead and ascended back to heaven, leaving a small band of disciples to carry on His work. Those men made an impact on the world which eventually transcended the significance of the Roman Empire itself. What they did was to establish groups of people who believed the Good News and committed their lives and resources to propagate it. Those groups were given a loose structure and called churches. Soon their influence began to affect the fabric of the communities where they were formed. Then it grew to affect large cities and eventually the whole Empire. This book is about the growth and development of first century churches.

The history book we call the New Testament is in two major sections. The first is concerned with the history of a Man--Jesus. The second is about the history of the movement He initiated--Christianity, especially the churches which are its visible form. The phenomenal growth of the churches was governed by principles which are clearly revealed in the record.

The Data Base--Original Documents

It is significant that we actually possess the original church growth documents. They are inspired by the Holy Spirit and profitable for our instruction and guidance. The sources for our examination of church growth in the first century are the New Testament documents themselves. In the rapidly expanding literature being produced on this subject, the major emphasis is on contemporary models of successful churches. Where principles are enunciated, they are sometimes based more on sociology than on theology. There is a scarcity of study material which uses these God-given documents as a data base. This book attempts to fill that gap.

10   BIBLICAL PRINCIPLES OF CHURCH GROWTH

The original documents are bulging with insights on how and why the early churches grew. Growth patterns emerge for us which are directly applicable and at the same time thoroughly Biblical. Both church planters and students of church growth will want to become familiar with the original documents and the apostolic practice described in them. As we study the New Testament in this light it takes on the character of a practical handbook for growing churches, rather than a theoretical textbook on ecclesiology.

The first document is Luke's narrative of the evangelism and church planting explosion after the resurrection of Christ (The Acts of the Apostles). Acts is followed by a series of 21 letters written to the newly established churches and to certain individuals. The letters contain advice and correction for their spiritual health and growth (Romans to Jude). The final document is apocalyptic in nature, but even it begins with an evaluation of seven individual churches in the province of Asia (Revelation).

From these documents we will examine the available data on the growth of six prominent churches. Beginning with the initial thrust of evangelism in each place and tracing the story as far as the New Testament record goes, principles will emerge which are just as useful today as they were nineteen hundred years ago.

The twin concepts of **church planting** and **church growth** come from the New Testament. Paul speaks of himself as a farmer when he says regarding the church at Corinth, "I planted .... you are God's field" (1 Cor. 3:6,9). The church was seen as a field in which had been planted the good seed of the Word of God. The planting operation determines the whole character of the growing garden or field. Preparing the soil, spacing the plants, watering, knowing the right time: all these were necessary to produce the fruit.

Modern church planting terminology comes from this passage. Paul was the planter; however, he emphasized that his work as planter on the practical level must not be confused with God's work on the spiritual level. The planter is responsible for human activity, but twice Paul reminds us that it is "God who causes the growth" (1 Cor. 6,7).

True Growth Comes from God

With so much emphasis today on the sociological and organizational aspects of church growth, we need to be reminded that true growth is spiritual and comes from God who gives life. Even back yard gardeners know that after all they may do it is God who gives botanical life and growth to the plants. At best they are merely encouragers of the principles of growth that God established at creation. This same principle applies in terms of spiritual life and growing churches.

Church growth is also described in terms of a growing human body whose head is Christ Himself (Eph. 4:16; Col 2:19). In both these passages the head directs the members of the body to facilitate growth. All the members have differing and necessary functions. While the "body" refers specifically to the universal body of Christ, each local church is a microcosm of the universal church.

I Will Build My Church

Another term which Paul used in describing his church growth activity is a metaphor of building a temple (1 Cor. 3:10). It echoes the prophetic statement that Paul the masterbuilder had the task of laying the foundation; as the church progressed, others would build on it. The foundation was most important because it determines the character of the building to be erected. The foundation Paul laid was the Truth of Jesus Christ upon which the church could stand firm. The church established on it was a "spiritual temple," God's building. Others were already building on the foundation, but there was only one masterbuilder.

Paul reminded them that others who built on the foundation he had laid were "sub-contractors" and should be careful to build using only durable materials which are in keeping with the Foundation (1 Cor. 3:10-15). Non durable materials like wood, hay and stubble symbolized anything out of keeping with Christ the Foundation. They refer to carnal and worldly methods used in an attempt to build His church. So the passage warns, "Let each man be careful how he builds" (v. 10).

For us who may be involved in assisting the growth

of a local church, this book will provide Biblical principles which are just as valid today as they were in New Testament times when they were first used and taught.

Chapter 1

THE CHURCH IN ANTIOCH
Evangelism, Key to Growing Churches

The church in Syrian Antioch is the first working model which contained the essential elements of a true New Testament church.[1] Our study of its remarkable growth will reveal important principles which are as effective today as they were in the first century. The potential for growth was placed there by God before there was a single believer in the city.

The city of Antioch lies a day's drive north of Jerusalem (300 miles). The name is still recognizable in the present day Turkish city of Antakya which occupies the site. The city was founded by Seleucus, one of the four generals who succeeded Alexander the Great three hundred years before Christ. He made it his military base from which to control Syria. By New Testament times it was the capital city in the Roman province of Syria and the third largest city in the world (pop. 500,000).

The location was ideal, on a fertile plain 18 miles up the Orontes River from the great harbor of Seleucia which accommodated large numbers of ships from all parts of the Mediterranean. Antioch was the terminus of the best caravan road East to the Orient which insured that the markets were filled with goods from the known world. It therefore became commercially prosperous and culturally diverse because of close contact with both Greek and Oriental culture.

Jews in large numbers had settled there from the beginning because they were promised equal privileges with Greeks. Like other Greek-speaking Jews they

---

[1] The church in Jerusalem is not a typical New Testament church because it did not contain any Gentile believers and was centered in the existing Temple.

were called Hellenists, and were more influenced by Greek culture than the Jews in Judea (Acts 6:1). The synagogues were open to interested Gentiles, many of whom were attracted to the one true God of the Jews and to their Scriptures which were in Greek. Neither Greek polytheism nor Oriental mysticism had anything comparable to offer.

No city in the Hellenistic world was so well suited to set off the evangelistic explosion of the first century. Its political and commercial importance gave it the ability to support Christian workers. Its cultural diversity helped it accept and adapt to new ideas. Its location on great trade routes made it strategically accessible to the whole of the Mediterranean world and the Middle East. Thus it was no accident that Antioch was to become the home of the first Gentile church mentioned in the New Testament and a strategic center of church growth.

Uniquely a Work Of God

We gain an important insight from this background, that God had uniquely prepared Antioch to be the host city of the church which would become the detonator for the evangelism explosion in the Roman empire. We will carefully note some helpful principles in the planting and growth of this new church, but the fact remains that God was at work long before the first convert. "Unless the Lord builds the house, they labor in vain who build it" (Psa. 127:1).

The first mention of Antioch in the New Testament is in connection with Nicolas, a Gentile from Antioch who had become a convert to Judaism. Like other Gentiles he had become attracted to the Scriptures and God of the Jews. Then he took a difficult step for any Gentile, becoming a proselyte Jew. The Bible picks up his story in Jerusalem where he evidently heard of Jesus and became a believer in Him.

His spirituality and wisdom were soon recognized so that when the church in Jerusalem needed men to look after the equitable distribution of food to the Greek-speaking widows who needed it Nicolas was among the seven chosen. He was specially described as being a "proselyte from Antioch," a man "of good reputation, full of the Spirit and of wisdom" (Acts 6:3-5).

PRINCIPLE: CHURCHES GROW BY THE INTENTIONAL USE OF ESTABLISHED RELATIONSHIPS AS BRIDGES TO EVANGELISM

Nicolas had three areas of established personal relationships which could be exploited for the purpose of evangelism in Antioch. First there were the Gentile friends and relatives with whom he had grown up. They were pagan idolaters, but might respond to the sincere witness of Nicolas when he returned to Antioch from Jerusalem and looked them up. The second group he knew in Antioch were in the synagogue where he had converted to Judaism. They already believed in God and the Scriptures, but did not yet know of the crucified and risen Messiah. Nicolas and other believers who started Christian work in Antioch were able to use these already established friendships as bridges to effective witnessing.

Nicolas had a third set of relationships which were important to the growth of the church in Antioch. It was with the believers in Jerusalem. He had become part of the church family with the result that the Jerusalem church took a special and continuing interest in him and other believers who moved with him to Antioch. When the Jerusalem believers heard that people were getting saved in Antioch, they responded by sending Barnabas to help them (Acts 11:22). Later the relationship between those two churches also stimulated help in the opposite direction when the believers in Antioch sent material relief to Jerusalem to help those threatened with famine (vv. 27-30).

Crossing the Bridges

We too can take advantage of "bridges." Like Nicolas we have relationships with non-Christians who are neighbors, business associates and social friends. The relational bridge allows us to "get across" to them with the Good News.[2] Perhaps we also have religious associates like Nicolas, whom we have met on our search for God. When he found the Truth, he had a "bridge" to take it across to them. He did this and they responded. We can too.

The third "bridge" was the relationship he established with believers in Jerusalem. They were perceptive enough to notice across the bridge a need for mature ministry there. They responded by sending Barnabas across to help them. The same bridge between Jerusalem and Antioch later was effective to offer help in the opposite direction. The Antioch believers became aware of a social need in Jerusalem and collected a large offering of money to help (Acts 11:27-30). Healthy church growth usually takes place in a context of relational "bridges." Taking advantage of these bridges is a primary growth principle. Alert Christians will identify the bridges and then use them.

God's time to use the bridges to church growth in Antioch was not far off. Another of the "seven deacons" in Jerusalem chosen along with Nicolas, was Stephen. He soon proved to be a powerful preacher of the Gospel. Opposition swirled around him from the orthodox Jews. They soon had him before the Council, and accused him of heresy. Stephen's great speech of defense led to his own death by stoning. A wave of persecution followed against all the believers in Jerusalem led by Saul of Tarsus (Acts 7:58--8:2). He is described as "ravaging the church, entering house after house and dragging off men and women" (Acts 8:3). The result was that hundreds of true believers were driven out of Jerusalem and went to settle in other cities.

PRINCIPLE: CHURCHES GROW WHEN ALL BELIEVERS TAKE SERIOUSLY THE COMMAND OF CHRIST TO BE WITNESSES

---

[2] An excellent resource book on this subject is THE MASTER'S PLAN FOR MAKING DISCIPLES, by Win and Charles Arn; Church Growth Press.

THE CHURCH IN ANTIOCH 17

Luke's narrative in Acts picks up the story of only one group of persecuted believers forced to leave Jerusalem; those who went to Antioch (Acts 11:l9-20). God moved them from Jerusalem to Antioch so that they would be strategically placed for church growth. They responded immediately to the new challenge God gave them by preaching Christ (v. 11:l9). They were simply obeying the mandate given to all believers to be "witnesses" (Acts 1:8). They began by witnessing to Jews just as they had done when they were still in Jerusalem. Witnessing was a priority in almost every conversation. With close cultural ties with the Jews they found it "natural" to reach out to them, pointing out that Jesus was both Lord and Messiah. Luke's record about what happened is simply a brief statement.

> So those who were scattered because of the persecution that arose in connection with Stephen made their way...to Antioch speaking the word to no one except to Jews alone (Acts 11:l9)

Three insights for church planting evangelists stand out. First, that the Antioch evangelists were not specialists or professionals. They comprised the whole spectrum of believers who happened to settle in that city. Every Christian was witnessing with no distinction between clergy and laity. To them witnessing was not a gift for a few paid specialists but a responsibility for all. One of the weak points in the growth strategy of the church today is that we are increasingly dependent on professionals to do the work of God.

The second insight is that they witnessed to those with whom they had the closest natural ties. Because they were all converts from Judaism, their strongest cultural links were with the Jews. Evangelism is most effective when aimed at those culturally closest to the evangelist. It is obvious that we can best communicate to those who are culturally closest to us. The third insight concerns what they did. They spoke "the word," that is, the Gospel. They began with the message, not with social help or reform. In a day when there is heavy emphasis on the social implications of the Gospel and "winning the right to be heard" by social activity, this insight may be important.

Crossing Ethnic Lines

The outreach to the Jews in Antioch was only the beginning of the story. Among those believers who were forced out of Jerusalem and settled in Antioch were some of daring spirit. They were believing Jews who had originally come from Cyprus and Cyrene. These were men like Simeon Niger and Lucius, both of whom became leaders in the Antioch church and were from Cyrene in North Africa (Acts 13:1). There were also men from the island of Cyprus although no names are indicated. Barnabas who was a Cypriot (Acts 4:36) did come to Antioch later, but was not part of the group forced to flee Jerusalem.

The giant step forward that these men took was to preach the Good News to Gentiles also--uncircumcised pagans. Perhaps to their surprise, there was an immediate response. Luke tells it,

> But there were some of them, men of Cyprus and Cyrene, who came to Antioch and began speaking to the *Greeks* also, preaching the Lord Jesus. And the hand of the Lord was with them, and a large number who believed turned to the Lord (Acts 11:20-21 *emphasis mine*)

The Gentile Greeks evidently were ready to repent from their sin and turn to the Lord for salvation. It may well be that some of them had previous contact with Jews and the synagogues. It was revolutionary that they should become believers in Christ without becoming Jews first. Luke the historian has carefully explained God's plan in this with the programming of Peter's thinking to accept Gentiles as believers, the conversion story of Cornelius and the coming of the Holy Spirit on the Gentiles (Acts 10). This was followed by Peter's explanation of it to the Jerusalem leaders after which "They glorified God saying, 'Well then, God has granted to the Gentiles also the repentance that leads to life'" (Acts 11:18). At this point Luke introduces the Antioch story as an example of Gentile outreach by Jewish believers.

Cross-Cultural Outreach

The significant insight here is that their evangelistic outreach broke new ground in presenting Christ to people outside of their own culture. Their willingness to move to the unploughed fields of pagan Greeks was to risk misunderstanding by more traditional Jewish Christians. They would have known this, but probably did not fully realize that they were raising what became the most critical issue in the life of the first century church: that Gentiles could become true believers without also identifying themselves as Jews. But issue or no issue, they were doing what many modern day churches are failing to do--reaching out to peoples of other cultures in their community. These Jewish Christians were not nearly as concerned about the social risk as they were for the souls of lost Gentiles. They were pioneers in cross-cultural evangelism.

Burning zeal for the lost of another cultural background is often missing in our churches. Inner city congregations have been denuded by "white flight" when the neighborhood changed character. Predominantly white churches often ignore the influx of Asian or Hispanic peoples to their communities. Evangelical whites in North America have not, as a rule, practiced what they preach. The Antioch model shows us that to be Biblical "there is neither Jew nor Greek...for you are all one in Christ Jesus" (Gal. 3:28).

God's Approval

God's approval of their cross-cultural witness is clearly stated. "And the hand of the Lord was with them, and a large number who believed turned to the Lord" (Acts 11:21). The "hand of the Lord" is a common Old Testament figure of speech indicating the power of God (eg. Isa. 59:1; 66:14). As the Antioch believers witnessed of their salvation, God added His power to their words so that pagan Greeks were turning to the Lord. When God's people are obedient to Him, He stretches out His powerful hand. "Behold the Lord's hand is not so short that it cannot save" (Isa. 59:1). Their obedience in cross-cultural witness was the key to the cornucopia of the Lord's hand. What a lesson for us who worship in ethnic evangelical ghettos.

PRINCIPLE: YOUNG CHURCHES GROW WHEN ACTIVELY ASSISTED BY MATURE CHURCHES

News of Antioch soon reached Jerusalem. Although the Jerusalem church neither planned nor directed the evangelism in Antioch, they acted when they heard of the developments there. They wanted to be sure that what was happening was of God, and if it was they wanted to help. Note their response and the reason for it.

> And the news about them reached the ears of the church at Jerusalem, and they sent Barnabas off to Antioch. Then when he had come and witnessed the grace of God, he rejoiced and began to encourage them all with resolute heart to remain true to the Lord, for he was a good man and full of the Holy Spirit and of faith. And considerable numbers were brought to the Lord (Acts 11:22-24).

The Jerusalem church was concerned about what was happening three hundred miles away. At considerable expense they sent Barnabas who had both spiritual discernment to assess the situation and the gift of encouragement to help where needed. These two attributes are indicated in Luke's description of Barnabas, "full of the Holy Spirit and of faith." He had spiritual discernment to perceive that it was God who was working through the believers in Antioch. Also he had faith to believe that the local church there was going to grow and bear fruit. It was a good investment in time and energy.

He was an outstanding example of sacrificial generosity because he sold his land and laid the money at the apostle's feet (Acts 4:36,37). His largeness of heart was demonstrated later when he alone believed Saul's story about his conversion and persuaded the Jerusalem leaders to receive him (Acts 9:26,27). His spiritual perception matched his selfless giving. Jerusalem's choice of Barnabas for the Antioch mission was a good one.

When he arrived in Antioch, Barnabas was not

THE CHURCH IN ANTIOCH

deterred because they were evangelizing in non-traditional ways. Instead, "he rejoiced and began to encourage them all with resolute heart to remain true to the Lord" (Acts 11:23). The traditional ways of doing things in Jerusalem did not blind a spiritually perceptive Barnabas to the possibility that God might work in other ways.

Many of us today lack the faith to believe that God may be pleased to work outside the old familiar paths of our tradition. If Barnabas had insisted that the church in Antioch fall into line with the traditions of Jerusalem, the growth of the church would have been severely limited. He encouraged them to remain "true to the Lord." Loyalty to the Lord was the criterion, not the Jerusalem traditions. May God give us the faith of Barnabas.

PRINCIPLE: GROWING CHURCHES NEED A VARIETY OF GIFTS

Growth in the Antioch church was stimulated by another wise move of Barnabas. He was humble enough to see that he alone was not "God's gift to Antioch." He needed help and was willing to seek it. He had the gifts of discernment and encouragement which he used. "Considerable numbers (literally multitudes) were brought to the Lord" through his ministry, but they needed teaching which Barnabas realized could be provided better by someone else.

The Acts record is simple in the extreme: "He left for Tarsus to look for Saul" (Acts 11:25). Behind this statement lies the confidence that Barnabas had in Paul from earlier contacts in Jerusalem (Acts 9:26,27). Barnabas knew that Paul had a special call from God to bear the Lord's Name to Gentiles (Acts 9:15). He knew too that Paul was a fearless witness and had gone to Tarsus in Cilicia (v. 30). He probably had reports that Paul was involved in a church planting ministry which seems evident from the record (Acts 15:23). It at least indicates that there were churches of Gentiles in Cilicia and the assumption is that Paul was active in their planting.

Barnabas travelled 130 miles from Antioch to Tarsus and found Paul, an expensive and risky journey. The important lesson for us in this is that Barnabas was wise enough to call in a gifted teacher when the young church needed that gift. Too many church planting efforts are stunted because the initiator does not get qualified help in needed areas. Either he fails to clearly see the need or he fails to see that he himself cannot adequately fill the need. Growing churches need spiritual and wise leaders like Barnabas who have the wisdom to know when help is needed and the grace to seek it.

Gathering Together

For a year the two men "met with the church and taught considerable numbers" (Acts 11:26). An important church growth factor emerges here in Antioch--the necessity of physically gathering together. The term "met" indicates an actual meeting together of the believers and is usually translated "gathered together." Luke uses this term a number of times in Acts to refer to the body life of the local church (Acts 4:31; 11:26; 14:27; 15:6; 15:30; 20:7). Being together in one place gives the believers an opportunity to experience the oneness of the fellowship and the sense of belonging to the group.

The New Testament church is a called-out group from the hostile world.[3] The church is also the gathering of the believers with emphasis on their identity and togetherness.[4] Many modern churches emphasize the evangelistic work to an extent that leaves little if any room for the local church to be gathered together and gathered away from the world.

PRINCIPLE: CHURCHES GROW WHEN BELIEVERS ARE GIVEN SOLID BIBLE TEACHING

---

[3] Greek "ekklesia" (Acts 20:7)

[4] Greek "synagoge" (Jas. 2:2)

THE CHURCH IN ANTIOCH

The purpose for their gathering is clear--the essential need for teaching (Acts 11:26). Both Barnabas and Saul had seen a model of teaching in the Jerusalem church and they put this into practice in Antioch (Acts 2:42). What did they teach? Paul later mentioned that when he was in Syria (Antioch) that he had "preached the faith" (Gal. 1:21-23). "The faith" consisted of the great truths of the Gospel as they emerged from the Old Testament Scriptures and the teachings of the Lord Jesus.

Solid Biblical teaching is one of the most fundamental principles of any church building ministry. Yet it is surprising how many churches lack it. The Bible seems virtually replaced by other things. In some it is replaced by drama and celebration; in others, by a legalistic set of do's and don'ts; or by emphasis on ecstatic experience; or even by a constant repetition of the means of coming to faith in Christ. The first believers who continued in "the apostle's doctrine" provided the first listed reason for their meetings (Acts 2:42). Growing Christians need nourishing food. Growing healthy churches consist of growing Christians.

Prophets and Famine Relief

Help for the Antioch church from Jerusalem continued; this time prophets came to assist with their gifts.

> Now at this time some prophets came down from Jerusalem to Antioch. And one of them named Agabus stood up and began to indicate by the Spirit that there would certainly be a great famine all over the world. And this took place in the reign of Claudius. And in the proportion that any of the disciples had means, each of them determined to send a contribution for the relief of the brethren living in Judea. And this they did, sending it in charge of Barnabas and Saul to the elders (Acts 11:27-30).

The ministry of the New Testament prophets was mainly for "edification and exhortation and consolation" (1 Cor.14:3). They were men gifted to teach by direct revelation from God. The written New Testament was not available until the third century. Until that time God used prophets to reveal His will. They spoke on behalf of God to the believers. Occasionally they spoke of coming events, as in our passage; but their great ministry was to speak for God to the Church--edifying, exhorting, comforting.

They were known for their authoritative word from God. The church today may not have prophets in their strictly New Testament sense because we have the whole Word of God. But we still need men who take God's Word and speak with authority, "this is what God says." The church today is woefully lacking in such men.

Generosity, a Mark of Growth

Another insight emerging from this incident is that the Christians there responded to the material needs of their brothers and sisters 300 miles away. Every one contributed to the offering proportionately, according to his or her ability.

Growing churches are giving churches. This was not only true in New Testament Antioch, but is equally true in healthy churches today. When the famine struck (probably 46 A.D.), they were ready and sent the relief to Jerusalem. Note the care they took to handle the funds with integrity.

The Sacrifice of Prayer

The church which had begun because its founders were not afraid to reach out across cultural lines now extended its outreach to include other parts of the Roman world. In the months which followed the leadership developed. Presumably the five men mentioned in Acts 13:1 were the leaders, whose gifts were prophecy and teaching.

Now there were at Antioch, in the church that was there, prophets and teachers: Barnabas and Simeon who was called Niger, and Lucius of Cyrene, and Manaen who had been brought up with Herod the tetrarch and Saul. And while they were ministering to the Lord and fasting, the Holy

Spirit said, Set apart for Me Barnabas and Saul for the work to which I have called them. Then when they had fasted and prayed and laid their hands on them, they sent them away (Acts 13:1-3).

Some insight into church growth can be gained by noticing the activities of the elders in Antioch. Notice that they were "ministering (literally 'engaged in priestly service') to the Lord, and fasting." The elders of spiritual churches today will be marked in a similar way. Their spiritual health was evident in the fasting and ministering to the Lord. The word for ministering is that used of Old Testament priests whose responsibility it was to offer sacrifices (Heb. 10:11). Here were spiritual leaders engaged in offering the sacrifices of prayer and fasting to God. Fasting for the sake of intense and extended prayer is an almost unknown spiritual exercise in many evangelical circles today. Nothing is more important for spiritual vitality than the "effectual fervent prayer" of spiritual leaders. No weekend seminar under the direction of the most "successful" church growth specialists in America comes close to it.

A Sending Church

Note also that they were listening for the voice of God; when the Spirit indicated that they should set apart Barnabas and Paul, they acted. They had eyes for the world and were ready to respond when God marked out two of their own number for distant service. The church got together and laid their hands on the two men for the work to which God had called them. And then they were "sent" away to get started. Antioch became the "base" for the three great missionary journeys of Paul and his companions. The New Testament pattern for the sending of missionaries was established and Antioch was the model. The growing church had eyes for the world and became the sending church. No less should be said for growing local churches where we worship.

Averting Disaster

The last view of the Antioch church in the New

Testament concerns an incident that had all the potential for division which could have spread throughout the early church. The chronology of events has been much debated, but the facts are clear. Division is one of the most powerful weapons in Hell's arsenal for church destruction. Even well-meaning leaders can be duped into becoming its launchers. In this case it was no less than Peter the Apostle.

Paul and Barnabas had arrived in Antioch after the first "missionary journey" to Galatia. They gathered the church and reported how God had "opened the door of faith to the Gentiles" (Acts 14:27). While they were there, Peter came to visit Antioch from Jerusalem and enjoyed the fellowship of the Lord's Supper with the believers comprising both Jews and Gentiles (Gal. 2:12).

Then "certain men" from Jerusalem arrived, who taught that circumcision was necessary for salvation. When they saw that both circumcised and uncircumcised believers were meeting together in Antioch, they stayed away. Peter saw this and because he was afraid of what others in Jerusalem might say he withdrew from the Antioch communion. He was followed in his "hypocrisy" by the rest of the Jews there, even including Barnabas (Gal 2:12,13).

Disaster loomed, but Paul saved the situation by challenging Peter before them all, and exposing his sin of hypocrisy. He boldly affirmed that we are "justified by faith in Christ and not by works of the law" (Gal. 2:14-16). Peter accepted Paul's rebuke and when later the same issue was discussed in the Jerusalem council, he used the same reasoning in defense of the truth that Paul had used to rebuke him (Acts 15:7-11).

The principle here for the church planter is to beware of the inroads of possible division through compromise of the truth. Sometimes this may even come from highly respected leaders such as Peter. The shepherds of the local church will have to stand boldly and firmly for the truth as Paul did at Antioch. They should also be sure that the issues for which they make a bold stand are indeed the issues of truth and not simply tradition. Traditions may be expendable; truth never is.

THE CHURCH IN ANTIOCH 27

GROWTH INSIGHTS FROM ANTIOCH

1. Growth is uniquely a work of God 14
2. Established relationships are bridges to growth 15
3. Evangelism is a priority for every believer 16
4. Evangelism reaches across cultural boundaries 18
5. Mother churches invest in daughter churches 20
6. Church planters seek gifts they cannot provide 21
7. Team leadership promotes growth 22
8. Growing churches gather for solid Biblical teaching 22
9. A good name promotes community identification 23
10. Growing churches are giving churches 24
11. Issues are faced squarely and resolved 24
12. Growing church leaders have a vision for the world 25
13. Healthy churches become sending churches 25
14. A growing church can expect attack from Satan 25

Chapter 2

THE CHURCHES IN GALATIA
Developing a Church Growth Strategy

Paul and Barnabas started out from Antioch in Syria on their first missionary journey with a definite purpose in view. They were "commended to the grace of God for the work." When they arrived back at Antioch the "work" had been accomplished--the work of opening a "door of faith to the Gentiles" by evangelism and church planting (Acts 14:26,27). They could report after only two years away that four new churches had been planted--a remarkable achievement by any standard. This chapter points out some important insights into why they were able to accomplish what they did.

The journey began in 47 A.D. from Antioch of Syria. It took Paul and Barnabas first to the Island of Cyprus and then to the mainland cities of Attalia and Perga where they stopped briefly. From there they went over the Taurus mountains northwards to the city of Pisidian Antioch, the first of the four cities in which they established churches on the first missionary journey. These cities, including Iconium, Lystra and Derbe, are a cluster and are referred to as the "churches of Galatia" in the Epistle to the Galatians.[5]

Pisidian Antioch was originally in Phrygia, but incorporated into the Roman province of Galatia in B.C. 25. The emperor Augustus made it a Roman Colony for the Romanization of Pisidia to the South. Thus it was called Antioch toward Pisidia or simply Pisidian Antioch to distinguish it from Antioch in Syria. It also had a significant Jewish community with a large synagogue. The

---

[5]Most modern commentators agree, though the reader may wish to explore other theories in commentaries on Galatians.

synagogue and the colony status of the city probably explain why Paul chose to begin his Galatian evangelism there. The synagogue provided potential for evangelizing the God-fearing Gentiles in the city and the colony status gave it potential for evangelistic influence on the surrounding communities.

The site of Pisidian Antioch is on the outskirts of the modern Turkish town of Yalvac. Of interest to the New Testament student are the ruins of a very old church, beneath which lie the older ruins of a first century synagogue; almost certainly the very spot where Paul preached the message recorded in Acts 13. The archaeological work done at the site by Yale University in 1914 is only now being published.

The Biblical record of this church begins with Paul and Barnabas:

> ....They arrived at Pisidian Antioch and on the Sabbath day they went into the synagogue and sat down. And after reading of the Law and the Prophets, the synagogue officials sent to them saying, "Brethren if you have any word of exhortation for the people say it." And Paul stood up, and motioning with his hand, he said, "Men of Israel and you who fear God, listen:" (Acts 13:14-16).

Note that Paul first went to witness in the synagogue as he had done in Cyprus (Acts 13:5). Almost all of the larger cities in the Roman Empire had significant Jewish populations and therefore synagogues. Paul habitually made them his initial points of contact for two reasons. The first is that Paul as a highly educated Jewish teacher had an immediate acceptance in any synagogue much as a world class chess player would have in any local chess club. For Paul the synagogue was an open door to preach the Gospel from the Jewish Scriptures.

People Prepared for the Gospel

The other reason Paul went to the synagogues is that they contained Gentiles who were likely to be the most responsive to the Good News he was proclaiming. The primary worshippers in the synagogues were Jews who were known for their faith in the true God, their authoritative Scriptures and their hope of a coming Messiah. But many Gentiles were also there. They had become disillusioned with the idolatry of the Romans which was not only morally corrupt, but did not recognize a personal God or hope beyond death. In their search for truth they were attracted to what the Jews had; a personal God, authoritative Scriptures and high moral standards. They flocked to the synagogues to learn more. It was this group which became Paul's special **target audience**. They are called "God fearers" in the New Testament and Paul wisely saw them as a people who were uniquely prepared to receive the Gospel.

In Pisidian Antioch Paul took advantage of his unique opportunity and addressed them in particular. Note his salutation in the quote above. "Men of Israel **and you who fear God**, listen" (Acts 13:16, also v. 26 *emphasis mine*). Now note who responded to that sermon: "Many of the Jews and **God fearing proselytes** followed Paul..." (Acts 13:43 *emphasis mine*). These God-fearers were not only Paul's target audience for evangelism, they became the core group in all the churches Paul started. When later he told what had happened in Galatia he implied that it was God who had created this special opportunity having "opened the door of faith to the Gentiles" (Acts 14:27).

PRINCIPLE: CHURCH GROWTH EVANGELISTS SHOULD TARGET PREPARED PEOPLE TO WHOM THEY HAVE ACCESS

As a twentieth century application it might be suggested that evangelists go first to the synagogues. Hold it! The principle is not that we start in the synagogues, but that we start where the potentially receptive people are. Find the fields that are both accessible and "white unto harvest." Look for people within your reach who are hungry for God and thirsty for righteousness. Start there. Perhaps you have neighbors who want to study the Bible. Start a Bible study. Perhaps you are an alcoholic and you can reach those who are still in its grip. Go for it. Look for people whom God may have prepared - at your place of work, in the P.T.A., at the club or wherever. A dying church might have a serious group of seekers who are like the "God-fearers" of Paul's day. If God has prepared them to respond, the results may surprise you. Be an alert Christian and make use of such opportunities. Paul did.

Effective Preaching

The sermon that Paul delivered to the Jews and God-fearers of Antioch is a masterpiece of evangelistic preaching (Acts 13:16-47). Note that his approach was through the media of preaching and not just waiting for his lifestyle as a Christian to take effect. In the strategy of God preaching was, and still is, an effective means of evangelism. John the Baptist used it. So did the Lord Jesus. Peter, Stephen, Philip and Paul all made preaching their primary tool of evangelism. Down through history God has been pleased to use "the foolishness of the message preached to save those who believe" (1 Cor 1:21). Preaching has never gone out of vogue.

Preaching for Growth

Some features of the message that Paul preached in the synagogue of Pisidian Antioch are well worth noting and may be applied by evangelistic preachers today. First it was thoroughly Biblical. He quoted from four different passages of Scripture and explained them. Second, it was Christ-centered. He spoke of the prophecies of Christ in the Old Testament, the coming of Christ, the rejection and death of Christ and of His resurrection. Third, it was related to both the felt needs and the real need of the audience. The keenest felt need of the God-fearers was to know God. It was for that reason that they had come to the synagogue. Their real need was that they lacked forgiveness of sin, so Paul preached, "through Him forgiveness of sins is proclaimed to you" (Acts 13:38).

The fourth thing about Paul's evangelistic preaching in Acts 13 is that it was suited to the cultural context of the audience. Included in the cultural millieu were such things as authoritarian government, low moral standards, good education, pre-eminence of rationalism, religious polytheism, etc. Many were seeking intelligent answers to life's great questions. Paul therefore leads these educated Jews and Greeks logically through the history of God's dealing with His people in the Old Testament. He reminds them of the promise that from the descendants of David the Messiah would come (Acts 13:22-23). Then he declared that "God has brought to Israel a Savior, Jesus." Though He was rejected and crucified by the Jewish leaders, there was incontrovertible evidence that He was really Messiah because God raised Jesus from the dead, which was attested by many witnesses. Paul adapted his message to the cultural background of his hearers. The modern word for this is contextualization.

Preaching For A Decision

One further feature of Paul's evangelism in Pisidian Antioch is that he preached to gain a decision. Not only did he tell them that through the risen Savior forgiveness of sins was available, but he specifically warns them with a solemn quote from the prophet Habakkuk that their response was urgent (Acts 13:41). Evangelistic preaching which expects a decision is less commonly heard today from evangelical pulpits than in the early part of this century. Perhaps we are making a mistake by a "low key" approach.

Results

The immediate result in Pisidian Antioch was that "many" of the Jews and the God-fearers followed Paul to hear more. He urged them to continue in the grace of God; that is, to understand salvation by grace on the same basis for both Jew and Gentile (Acts 13:43). One week later there were so many Gentiles gathered to hear Paul that the Jews became jealous and started contradicting and blaspheming. To this Paul and Barnabas replied that they would then turn from the Jews and preach to the Gentiles, because even the prophet Isaiah declared that the Servant of Jehovah would bring "salvation to the ends of the earth." Paul and Barnabas applied that Scripture to their own ministry in Pisidian Antioch. Many Gentiles responded by believing in God's grace for salvation (vv. 42-48).

A Church is Planted

Another result of their evangelistic preaching was the formation of a group of new Christians meeting separately from the synagogue. They were eagerly listening to Paul and Barnabas and witnessing to their friends. They were so excited about their faith that "the Word of the Lord was being spread through the whole region" (Acts 13:49). We can note here that Paul"s strategic choice of Pisidian Antioch (because it was both a Roman colony and had a synagogue) worked well on both counts. The synagogue gave him the "in" to the God-fearers and the colony status gave the converts the opportunity to reach the surrounding district.

A third result of their preaching was that the opposing Jews used their considerable influence to persuade the leading women and men of the city to run the evangelists out of the district. Paul and Barnabas shook the dust off their feet as they left the city in protest against the unbelief of their fellow Jews who had so strongly rejected the message of Jesus the Messiah.

Note, however, that though the evangelists were driven out, they had left behind them a happy, growing congregation of disciples--exactly what they had set out to do. Luke records that the disciples there were continually filled with joy and with the Holy Spirit (Acts 13:52). A church had been planted.

Iconium

When Paul and Barnabas shook off the dust of Antioch from their feet in protest against the unbelief of the Jews, they were not on their way home. They went seventy miles east to the next important city along the major highway through southern Galatia, Iconium. It is still a large city in central Turkey with almost the same name, Konya. Here, just as in Pisidian Antioch, they went into the synagogue and took the

THE CHURCHES IN GALATIA   35

opportunity to speak. They repeated their strategy which had been effective in a similar situation. Consider:

> And it came about that in Iconium they entered the synagogue of the Jews together, and spoke in such a manner that a great multitude believed, both of Jews and of Greeks. But the Jews who disbelieved stirred up the minds of the Gentiles, and embittered them against the brethren. Therefore they spent a long time there speaking boldly with reliance upon the Lord, who was bearing witness to the word of His grace, granting that signs and wonders be done by their hands. But the multitude of the city was divided; and some sided with the Jews and some with the apostles. And when an attempt was made by both the Gentiles and the Jews with their rulers, to mistreat and stone them, they became aware of it and fled to the cities of Lycaonia, Lystra and Derbe and the surrounding region (Acts 14:1-6).

PRINCIPLE: EFFECTIVE EVANGELISTS CAN EXPECT POWERFUL OPPOSITION

Luke points out the way they presented the Gospel. They spoke "in such a manner" that a great multitude believed, both of Jews and Greeks." Their sincerity and intensity in preaching was complimented by the power of God. Many were converted. But, as is often the case, the power of God was challenged by the power of Satan. Many had "believed" but others "disbelieved"--a word which indicates not just unbelief, but opposition to belief, or disobedience (1 Cor. 14:2). These "stirred up the minds of the Gentiles and embittered them against the brethren."

Power Encounter

Something new in the ministry of Paul and Barnabas then occurred. God granted that "signs and wonders" be done by their hands (1 Cor. 14:3). These attesting miracles had been performed by Peter, the Apostles, Stephen and Philip, but up to this time they had not marked the ministry of Paul and Barnabas. As they gave witness to the "word of His grace," God confirmed their witness with signs. Sometimes, but not always, God granted signs to authenticate his Message. They were not a part of the Gospel, and then, as now, spiritual gifts were given "to each one individually just as He wills" (1 Cor. 12:11).

Paul later refers to signs and wonders three times (Acts 15:12; Rom. 15:19; 2 Cor. 12:12). Perhaps what is remarkable is that something as spectacular as miracles received so little attention by Paul in his New Testament writings.

Jewish reaction to the power of the Gospel was immediate. They used their influence in the city to turn as many Gentiles as possible against the new believers. In a short time the whole city was polarized in relation to the Christians and their Gospel. The opponents schemed to kill Barnabas and Paul by stoning, but they learned of the plan and fled before they became martyrs. The effectiveness of their preaching guaranteed opposition. Many believed and many actively disbelieved.

The Gospel is still a message which evokes opposition. Today in North America stoning by religious interests would be a most unlikely reaction, but other forms of opposition are common; these could include rejection by family, ridicule from the scientific community and accusations of bigotry and narrow mindedness from civil liberties organizations. Although Paul and Barnabas knew that opposition was to be expected, they did not compromise or weaken the Gospel message in order to avoid it. The very human tendency to compromise the truth of the Gospel to minimize personal pressure is as real today as it was then.

Lystra

Escaping from Iconium, Paul and Barnabas went south about 24 miles to Lystra, a small town in the heart of a district of Galatia called Lycaonia. Lystra was a Roman colony populated by Lycaonians who spoke

THE CHURCHES IN GALATIA 37

their own language. There does not seem to have been a synagogue and possibly Paul went to Lystra thinking that His Jewish opponents might not follow him. He was wrong. The story of the beginnings of this church is told by Luke in Acts 14:6-20. A few observations will provide some insights for us who seek to reach out with the Gospel during this age.

Luke's first statement is, "And there they continued to preach the Gospel" (Acts 14:7). Paul's tenacity of purpose stands out clearly. He had just been driven out of two Galatian towns with threats on his life, yet he "continued to preach the Gospel." He did not give up even though there was no synagogue. He adapted his strategy to the new situation and preached in the open air to any who would listen even though he probably had to use an interpreter.[6] His willingness to change his strategy to meet a different situation is an example to us. It reveals the heart of a true evangelist.

Getting the Ear of the Audience

One of the people in his audience became the instrument God used to gain the attention of the Lycaonian people in Lystra. Paul noticed him, a paraplegic, listening intently as he preached the Gospel. Somehow Paul perceived that the Spirit of God was at work in his heart. Perhaps it was a gift of spiritual insight, or perhaps simply a preacher's understanding of his audience. Sensitive preachers of the Gospel are often aware of those with whom God is working. Sometimes it is seen in the eagerness with which they are listening, or in the facial expression.

Paul saw that the cripple had faith "to be made well," or, as the margin says "to be saved" (Acts 14:9). There may be some debate as to whether his faith was first toward physical healing or toward salvation from sin. In either case God was the object of his faith and the result of it was both spiritual salvation and physical healing. The "miracle" of the new birth was the greater of the two. However the miracle of healing had an important purpose beyond the exper-

---

[6] It appears that they spoke Lycaonian (Acts 14:11)

ience of the man which was not at first apparent.

God used the dramatic effect of the physical healing to capture the attention of the city of Lystra. The open air crowd was electrified when Paul suddenly shouted to the paraplegic, "'Stand upright on your feet,' and he leaped up and began to walk" (Acts 14:10). At first the townspeople thought that the performers of the miracle were connected to one of their own local legends in which the gods Zeus and Hermes were supposed to have visited an old couple in Lystra many years before. They now assumed that Barnabas and Paul were Zeus and Hermes come back to Lystra (vv. 11,12). Suddenly the whole town was preparing for a big celebration over it.

Seizing the Opportunity

Paul and Barnabas did not at first know what the hubbub was all about because they did not understand the Lycaonian language. But when they saw the priest of the local temple of Zeus coming toward them with garlands to put on the missionaries as if they were gods, and oxen being led out to be sacrificed, they realized what was happening. They also realized that God had given them a wonderful opportunity to present the Gospel to the crowd of people that had gathered. The lesson for us is that they seized the opportunity when God gave it to them.

They began by tearing their garments as a dramatic way of saying "No, no, no!" to being honored as pagan gods. Then they rushed into the middle of the crowd to identify themselves as ordinary people. By this time everyone's attention was on them so they took the opportunity to preach the Gospel. In doing so there was some risk from the mob-like crowd, but the evangelists were willing to take it.

A Strategy for the Uncultured

Paul's message was again masterfully adapted to his audience in Lystra. The people were uncultured in the civilizations of Greece or Rome, nor did they know anything of the Jewish Scriptures or the true God. Paul began by introducing himself and Barnabas as ordinary men who were merely messengers of the true God, not gods to be worshipped. He explained the true God as the Creator of all things and the Controller of the nations of man. Though God had permitted nations to go in their own sinful ways, He had left a witness of His love for man by sending seasonal rains for man's harvest. Now God was giving them the good news of the Gospel through the missionaries (Acts 14:14-18).

The whole incident was skillfully turned into an evangelistic opportunity because Paul and Barnabas were alert and ready to seize it. The healing of the lame man caught the attention of the people. The mistaken identity of the missionaries for gods and the attempted sacrifice brought the crowds. Then they preached the Gospel in a way which was understandable to the people. He did not appeal to the prophecies of Jewish Scriptures (appropriate for Jewish audiences), but to the goodness of God the Creator. Church planting evangelists should be constantly ready to take the opportunities which God provides.

Timothy Converted at Lystra

There are no statistics given by Luke as to the number of people converted in Lystra, but the fact that Paul and Barnabas soon returned there to appoint elders in the church indicates that many converts were made (Acts 14:23). We can safely assume that one of them was Timothy whom Paul calls "my true child in the faith" indicating that Paul was his spiritual parent (1 Tim 1:2). Two years later on his second missionary journey when Paul came to Lystra he found Timothy was a "disciple" with a reputation for Christian service in two cities. With their recommendation Paul invited him to join the missionary team in their church planting ministry (Acts 16:1-3; 2 Tim. 3:10,11).

The end of the first evangelistic thrust in Lystra came suddenly. Jews, offended by the Gospel of grace, followed Paul to Lystra and tried to kill him. They had enough influence to incite the non-believers of Lystra to stone Paul after which they dragged him out of the city and left him for dead. The disciples who came out to claim the body saw Paul revive and go with them into the city (Acts 14:19,20). This is probably a testimony to the physical stamina which Paul possessed. The very next day he travelled sixty miles to Derbe.

The Brandmarks of Jesus

The wounds inflicted by the stones left scars on Paul's body. Paul mentioned them when he later wrote to the believers in Lystra and other Galatian churches, "Let no one cause trouble for me, for I bear on my body the brandmarks of Jesus" (Gal. 6:17). He considered those scars to be the identifying marks of his service for Christ. Just as the false teachers were claiming circumcision as a "mark" of their keeping the law of Moses, so Paul was claiming the scars on his own body as the marks of bondservice to his Lord. Probably there is no better "certificate" for the true evangelist than the evidence of his suffering for Christ in the ministry. Paul never sought "scars," about which he could boast, but he accepted the pain which brought them as part of the price of serving God. He was not trying to be a martyr, but rather to be faithful. Not many of us have much to show!

Derbe

The last of the Galatian cities visited by Paul and Barnabas on their missionary journey was Derbe. It was about sixty miles east of Lystra and the smallest city of the four evangelized. Luke only mentions two facts about the work of Barnabas and Paul in Derbe. First, that they preached the Gospel there (Acts 14:21). Preaching the Gospel was the primary thrust in each of the four Galatian cities. Luke wants to leave us with absolutely no doubt that the activity of preaching and the subject of the Gospel were the important things--not social work, not entertainment, not miracles.

The second thing mentioned about the beginning of the Derbe church is that they "made many disciples" (Acts 14:21). The people who had responded to the preaching of the Gospel were now discipled, taught and trained like apprentices so they could properly function in the church and in the world. Perhaps in our day there is a greater emphasis on making "converts" than on making "disciples." Ultimately the progress of church growth will depend on disciples.

PRINCIPLE: CHURCH GROWTH STRATEGY IS CLEARLY SUMMARIZED IN SCRIPTURE

Paul's strategy of church growth is nowhere summarized more clearly than in Luke's record of his return journey from Derbe back through the four cities of Galatia where churches had been planted. It is the most concise statement on the strategy of evangelism and church planting in the New Testament.

> And after they had preached the gospel to that city and had made many disciples, they returned to Lystra and to Iconium and to Antioch, strengthening the souls of the disciples, encouraging them to continue in the faith and saying, "Through many tribulations we must enter the kingdom of God." And when they had appointed elders for them in every church, having prayed with fasting, they commended them to the Lord in whom they had believed (Acts 14:21-23).

As they returned, Paul and Barnabas visited the churches again even though they had been forced out of all except Derbe. The newly planted churches needed spiritual growth and direction, and Paul was willing to take risks in order to see that the needs were met. Three major points of Paul's strategy are mentioned in these verses related to the health and growth of young believers in the Galatian churches.

First, they preached the Gospel (Acts 14:21). Second, they trained the new believers to be disciples. Two important parts of this are clear in this passage. They *strengthened* the disciples--that is, they built them up in the knowledge of the Truth (v. 22). Solid Biblical teaching is vital to the growth of God's people who are young in the faith. Paul hoped to prepare them for the challenge of false teaching which soon "disturbed" them (Gal. 1:7). Another part of the training process was that they *encouraged* the new believers to "continue in the faith"-- that is, to live out the faith in the neighborhood and marketplace (v. 22). The faith was to be made visible in the practical display of the character of Christ in the believer's lives. It was an extension of their initial faith in Him.

A third aspect of the training of new believers was that they *prepared* them for coming trials. Since trials cannot be escaped, they must be expected and thus prepared for. These discipleship techniques are just as important today: to know the Truth, to live the Truth and to suffer for the Truth.

Structuring Church Leadership

The third major point of Paul's strategy has to do with providing leadership structure for the community of believers. They appointed elders in every church (Acts 14:23). Even though the Galatian churches were all under two years old, the missionaries appointed those responsible for the government and shepherding which every church needs. Leadership is most important for every local church. In the pattern of the church in the New Testament the elders are consistently mentioned in the plural. The church planters appointed elders as a team of leaders in each church. The church was then left with structure for leadership which could perpetuate itself without further apostolic direction. Finally the church planters let go the control themselves. They did not stay on as the indispensable hierarchy. When they "prayed with fasting" they "commended" (literally "handed over") the new elders to the Lord.

A Viable Church in a Hostile World

We can hardly over-emphasize the importance of the basic principles of church planting mentioned here. The thrust of the apostles was directed toward producing strong well-taught believers, formed into structured communities called churches. The emphasis was specifically in producing a viable local church in a hostile world.

A modern example where these basics were its main thrust is the church in China between 1949 and 1989.

THE CHURCHES IN GALATIA 43

Without buildings, social programs or media opportunities the church has grown fifty times over from one million to probably fifty million. The key? Effective Gospel witnessing by all believers, heavy emphasis on personal discipleship and strong house churches which provided strength and encouragement in a hostile society. They are New Testament churches in the twentieth century.

Paul's Letter to the Four Galatian Churches

After re-visiting the four new Galatian churches, Paul and Barnabas went back to the church in Antioch of Syria from which they had been commended to the work of God. They gathered the church and reported on the results of their evangelistic thrust into Galatia.

And from there they sailed to Antioch from which they had been commended to the grace of God for the work that they had accomplished. And when they had arrived and gathered the church together, they began to report all things that God had done with them and how He had opened the door of faith to the Gentiles. And they spent a long time with the disciples (Acts 14:26-28).

Paul and Barnabas maintained a continuing relationship with their commending church. We do not know the extent to which this church supported them financially, but we do know that Paul and Barnabas demonstrated accountability in reporting everything that God had done with them. The new churches were an outgrowth of the one in Antioch. They too were autonomous and their structure consisted simply of recognized elders. But they were healthy, indigenous and growing.

The Danger of Legalism

While Paul and Barnabas were still in Antioch two things happened which affected the churches in Galatia. Both of these were moves by the Jewish legalists. First there came a report from Galatia that some of these had infiltrated the churches there and were teaching the believers that it was necessary to practice circumcision in addition to believing in the Gospel. They charged that Paul was not a true apostle; that his Gospel of grace was deficient, and that it led to unholy living. Paul reacted sharply to this by writing the Galatian letter in which he carefully refutes all three of the charges in some of the strongest language of the New Testament, e.g. "If any man is preaching a gospel contrary to that which you received, let him be accursed" (Gal. 1:9).

Paul's concern was that truth was being distorted and the church was being disturbed (Gal. 1:7). He could not bear the thought that the churches he had planted would be poisoned by these false teachers when his body still bore the scars of what it had cost him (Gal. 6:17). So in his letter to them he draws sharp lines between revealed truth and legalistic error. He defends his own apostleship against their false claims (Gal. 1--2). He made crystal clear the difference between grace and law (Gal. 3--4). He also stresses the importance of holy living based on the Gospel of grace (Gal 5--6). All this was to restore the equilibrium of churches unbalanced by the false teaching; that is the heart of a successful church planter.

Doctrinal issues in the church affect its growth. If they are improperly handled there will soon be division and dissension. In the Galatian problem of legalism, they went right to the source of the problem in Jerusalem, reached a conclusion and then informed the believers. The result was growth. *So* the churches "were increasing in number daily" (Acts 16:5). Too many churches with growing potential are smothered by the smoke of smoldering issues.

The Fruit of Church Planting
Church Planters

It must have been gratifying to Paul when visiting the Galatian churches, after being away more than a year, to witness remarkable growth both in the number of churches and in the lives of the believers. Timothy was an outstanding young man in Lystra who had almost certainly been converted when Paul was there before. On his second journey Paul found him "well spoken of by the brethren in Lystra and Iconium" (Acts 16:1,2). His spiritual impact was being felt in two cities. He saw Timothy's potential and wanted him to join their church-planting team. The brethren evidently agreed and Timothy became a lifelong companion and help to Paul and his ministry.

Training Leaders, a Major Principle

Timothy's conversion, discipleship training, and growth in Christian life and service as a future leader is one of the most valuable insights we get from the story of the young church in Lystra. Paul trained potential leaders right from the beginning of the young church. And he used the church as the training ground for them. Paul was not simply training Timothy to "take over," he was training Timothy to train "faithful men" who would be able to train "others also" (2 Tim. 2:2). Leadership was vital and the provision of training future leaders from the very beginning was also vital. Nothing is more vital to church growth than leadership and nothing is more vital to leadership than training it.

Growing churches in the New Testament produced their own leaders from within. They had nowhere else to turn. Leaders came from those who had been saved and discipled in the new churches. The on-the-job training in a local church is most valuable because it is so practical. Formal classroom training offers many advantages, but it can never replace the value of practical involvement. This is particularly true when existing leaders are monitoring the training of younger men. Healthy growing churches produce men who are best able to participate in the planting of more healthy churches.

Keeping in Touch

One final insight into Paul's success in Galatia is that he continued to keep in touch with the young churches to ensure their spiritual growth. We have seen that during the first missionary journey he and Barnabas returned a second time to each church to strengthen the Christians. Later, when Paul was in Syrian Antioch, he heard of the "invasion" of legalistic teachers and responded by writing the letter we call GALATIANS. Shortly after that his concern for their welfare shows up again.

> And after some days Paul said to Barnabas, "Let us return and visit the brethren in every city in which we proclaimed the word of the Lord, and see how they are" (Acts 15:36).

The first reason for Paul's second missionary journey was the spiritual welfare of the Galatian churches. He had the heart of a spiritual father for his children. Their healthy growth and development was of first importance. Personal cost, risk and difficulty were all secondary. With Silas as a companion he began the long journey on foot. The Galatian churches of Derbe, Lystra, Iconium and Antioch needed the reinforcement of instruction and exhortation. No one could better provide it than the church planter himself. Paul knew this and paid the price to do it. The commentary in Acts speaks for the wisdom of Paul's action. "So the churches were being strengthened in the faith and were increasing in number daily" (Acts 16:5).

Nor did Paul's contact end there. On his third missionary journey when he set out from Antioch of Syria, the first place he went was to Galatia, and for the same reason, "Strengthening all the disciples" (Acts 18:23). When he wrote First Corinthians in about 55 A.D., he mentioned to them that he had instructed the churches in Galatia to collect money for the poor in Jerusalem (1 Cor. 16:1). The clear implication is that there must have been continuing contact. Paul's great accomplishments in bigger cities never overshadowed his love and care for the churches in Galatia. As spiritual father, he never ceased caring for his spiritual children.

THE CHURCHES IN GALATIA   47

GROWTH INSIGHTS
FROM THE CHURCHES OF GALATIA

PISIDIAN ANTIOCH

1. Targeting people prepared for the Gospel   30
2. Preaching the Gospel in the context of
   the audience   32
3. Preaching to gain a decision   33

ICONIUM

4. Repeating previously successful strategy   34
5. Power encounter with the enemy   35
6. Maintaining a balance between courage
   and wisdom   35

LYSTRA AND DERBE

7. Grasping cross-cultural evangelistic
   opportunities   37
8. Different strategies for different people   38
9. The marks of preaching in a hostile world   40

GALATIAN CHURCHES
ESTABLISHED AND STRENGTHENED

10. Paul's strategy for establishing new
    churches   41
11. Leadership structure   42
12. Combatting the danger of legalism   43
13. The planted church produces a church
    planter   44
14. Training leaders   45
15. Continuing care   45

Chapter 3

THE CHURCH IN PHILIPPI
Growth Stimulated By Love

The story of church growth in the city of Philippi portrays perhaps the most successful church in the New Testament. Certainly to Paul it was personally the most rewarding. Of no other church did Paul write in such warm terms: e.g. "I thank my God in all my remembrance of you, I have you in my heart, My beloved brethren whom I long to see, my joy and crown" (Phil. 1:3,7: 4:1). Their spiritual maturity and balance delighted the Apostle. No other church cared so deeply for him. One evidence of this was that they repeatedly sent gifts for his ministry and personal needs right up to the end of his life.

The establishment of a church in Philippi marked a forward step in the strategic advance of the Gospel. It became the first church on the continent of Europe and was destined to play an important role in the progress of worldwide Christianity. Paul, however, could not yet see it in that broad historical setting. He saw it simply as a foothold for the Gospel in an unevangelized province, Macedonia.

Philippi was a gold mining town called Krenides in classical Greek times. Philip, father of Alexander the Great, enlarged it and named it Philippi after himself in 356 B.C. He bankrolled many of his ambitious projects from the then diminishing gold mines. In Roman times (42 B.C.) Philippi was the site of two battles after the assassination of Julius Caesar. From these Augustus emerged as the Emperor. Augustus gave Philippi the status of "colony" in honor of his victory there. The Egnatian Road which crossed the Balkan Peninsula had its eastern terminus at Philippi. The city was described by Luke as a "leading city of the district of Macedonia" which made it a prime target for the initial thrust of the Gospel in the province (Acts 16:12). Its importance was more military than commercial, however, which may explain why there were so few Jews living there.

Luke summarizes the means by which God led Paul there in a striking way. In broad quick strokes of the pen he brings Paul from Galatia to Macedonia. It is as if he avoids detail in Paul's approach to Philippi deliberately so as to accentuate the details of what happened after he arrived. Note Luke's summary.

> And they passed through the Phrygian and Galatian region having been forbidden by the Holy Spirit to speak the word in Asia; and when they had come to Mysia, they were trying to go into Bithynia, and the Spirit of Jesus did not permit them; and passing by Mysia, they came down to Troas. And a vision appeared to Paul in the night: A certain man of Macedonia was standing and appealing to him, and saying, "Come over to Macedonia and help us." And when he had seen the vision, immediately we sought to go into Macedonia, concluding that God had called us to preach the Gospel to them (Acts 16:6-10).

Paul and Silas were on the second missionary journey and had just revisited the churches in southern Galatia which they planted on the first journey. Timothy had joined them in Lystra bringing their team strength up to three. He contributed some youthful zeal to the team and the wisdom that his Greco/Hebrew parents gave him as an inheritance. Paul gained a companion with whom he would later join in writing six of his letters and to whom he wrote two personally.

Spiritual Sensitivity to God's Guidance

At this point the evangelical sights of the three evangelists were set on the province of Asia to the West. The Roman province of Asia occupied almost all of western Asia Minor in Paul's day. It included the districts of Phrygia, Lydia and Mysia and influential cities such as Ephesus, Sardis, Smyrna and Pergamos. Paul's church planting strategy for extending the frontiers of the kingdom of God into this province was perfect. Asia was needy, nearby and influential.

THE CHURCH IN PHILIPPI

But God said "no." As they started out across the province they were "forbidden by the Holy Spirit to speak the Word" there. The effect of this is that though the trio passed right across Asia they did not preach the Gospel there. Half way across, and near the border of Bithynia they tried to go north to Bythinia on the Black Sea, but "the Spirit of Jesus did not permit them." Again they had made a move toward a sensible field, and again the Spirit blocked the way. Just how they were directed we are not told, but it may have been by a strong inward impression which they sensed was from the Holy Spirit. Neither Asia to the west nor Bithynia to the north was allowed.

PRINCIPLE: GOD GUIDES SPIRITUALLY SENSITIVE PEOPLE

The important point for us in our day is that their common sense strategy was not God's purpose for them at that time. It may be easy from our perspective to look back and see why they should have gone to Philippi, but they were in the frustration of twice being told "no" and not yet having received clear guidance as to what they should do. In their frustration of being held back there is a basic principle for us. It is their sensitivity to God's direction even when they were following a strategy which was right in line with their commission. Church planters must never let their own plans supersede the "still small voice" of God. The pragmatism of church growth strategy should never replace the daily dependence on the Spirit of the Lord who is building His church. We are His workmen not His architects.

Audio Visual from God

The trio continued northwest until they arrived at Troas, a seaport on the Aegean coast. They were still in a quandary as to where to go. Luke evidently joined them there in Troas for the Acts narrative begins using the word "we" instead of "they" (Acts 16:10). His abilities as physician, poet, geographer and historian would be of immense value. (Luke wrote one of the Gospels and Acts.) And his being a Gentile would add an ethnic advantage to a team focused on establishing Gentile churches.

Presumably the four men were waiting on God for His direction. Just at this point God intervened. Paul had a night vision of a man from Macedonia beckoning to him and saying "Come over to Macedonia and help us." All four of them then conferred on the matter and they agreed that this was the direction for which they were waiting. Macedonia was to be the site of their next church planting effort.

A couple of good insights arise from this incident. First it was not a one man show. Paul had the vision, but it was all four of the team members who concluded that God had called them to preach the Gospel in Macedonia (Acts 16:10). Even Paul needed and sought the wise counsel of fellow workers. He was a strong leader, but not autocratic. As such he brought his team into the decision-making process. Note also that having ascertained the call of God, they immediately made plans to go to Macedonia. "Obedience is not obedience at all unless it is immediate."

Note one more thing. God called them to a Roman province, Macedonia. They selected one city in that province which was Philippi. Luke tells us why.

> Therefore putting out to sea from Troas we ran a straight course to Samothrace and on the day following to Neapolis; and from there to Philippi, which is a leading city of the district of Macedonia, a Roman colony; and we were staying in this city for some days (Acts 16:11-12).

Philippi was both a leading city of Macedonia and it was a Roman colony. As a "leading city" on the "Via Egnatia" it was of social and geographical importance to their evangelistic plans. Its status as a Roman "colony" gave its citizens privileges, such as the right to vote in Rome, the capitol of the empire. The potential in this might have an impact on Rome itself in the days to come. Philippi was a wise choice.

THE CHURCH IN PHILIPPI 53

Beginnings in Philippi

The team was now made up of Paul the converted rabbi, Silas the trusted Jewish Christian from Jerusalem, Timothy the young disciple from Lystra and Luke the physician probably from Syrian Antioch. Together the Philippi team possessed many excellent qualities which would contribute to the birth and growth of the new church. Three of them, Paul, Luke and Timothy, maintained close contacts with Philippi during the remainder of New Testament history.

They had sailed from Troas, via the Island of Samothrace and landed at Neapolis in Macedonia in only two days as the wind was with them. Then they proceeded eight miles directly inland to Philippi. It did not occur that they were the vanguard of the Christian invasion of Europe. They arrived there in obedience to God with the intent of establishing a living church of believers. God helped them do just that.

Observation and Planning

The first phrase in the narrative gives us a good insight for pioneer evangelism. "We were staying in this city (Philippi) for some days" (Acts 16:12). The emphasis is on the word "staying" and indicates that they found accommodation and quietly observed the people there. There is wisdom in unobtrusively sizing up a situation before the initial thrust is made. Every community has unique features about it which may affect the methodology used. Philippi, like Lystra, had no synagogue in which to make initial contacts. A new situation needed a new approach. No doubt much prayer went into those days of observation listening and formulating. Their strategy of prayerful observation is a good one for pioneer evangelists to follow in our day.

Philippi had a tiny Jewish population, not enough to have a synagogue, but it did have a "place of prayer," like a number of cities in the Roman world. These were often walled enclosures by a river in which the local Jews met to pray in the spirit of Psalm 137. "By the rivers of Babylon, there we sat down and wept when we remembered Zion." The four evangelists heard of, looked for and found such a place in Philippi. The record is worth reading for it introduces the key person prepared by God for the initial evangelization of Philippi--Lydia.

> And on the Sabbath day we went outside the gate to a river side where we were supposing that there would be a place of prayer; and we sat down and began speaking to the women who had assembled. And a certain woman named Lydia, from the city of Thyatira, a seller of purple fabrics, a worshipper of God, was listening; and the Lord opened her heart to respond to the things spoken by Paul. And when she and her household had been baptized, she urged us, saying, "If you have judged me to be faithful to the Lord, come into my house and stay." And she prevailed upon us (Acts 16:13-15).

She was, interestingly enough, a woman from Asia where Paul and Silas had been stopped from preaching a couple of weeks before. She was a business woman who sold fabric colored with a special purple dye manufactured in her home city. She is identified as a "worshipper of God" which means at least that she was a Gentile with a hunger for God and seeking to find Him through Judaism. Her love for God and His servants opened the door.

God at Work

Paul took the opportunity to speak to the women at the river about the Lord Jesus Christ as the promised Messiah. As he spoke God opened Lydia's heart to the truth. She responded by faith in Christ, along with those of her household who were with her. They were then baptized right there as a witness to their faith in Christ who died and rose from the dead. Baptism was the public ceremony to mark their conversion. God who had called the evangelists there had prepared the heart of Lydia to respond to the spoken Word.

This little bit of history reminds us again that God was the principle worker and the evangelists were working with Him. Church planters today should not forget this truth. God sends and guides His servants to

THE CHURCH IN PHILIPPI   55

be at the right place at the right time. God opens the hearts of the hearers to receive the salvation which God Himself provided. Paul as the servant of God simply took the opportunity God gave to preach the Good News. Lydia and her household simply took the opportunity to believe the Good News. True church growth is all of God. The Lord declared "I will build My church" (Matt. 16:18). Lydia and her household were the core group of the new church in Philippi.

The Hospitality Factor

Lydia not only displayed her faith by being baptized, she asked for the opportunity to entertain the four evangelists in her home. Her new faith in God was demonstrated by her love. She was eager to use her home and means to assist the establishment of the new church in Philippi. New converts often want to demonstrate their love for the Lord in practical ways. Church planters should find helpful outlets for the spiritual energy of new believers.

Paul and his three fellow workers seemed reticent at first to let her entertain them. She "prevailed" upon them when she linked her request to a demonstration of her faith in God. "If you have judged me to Be faithful to the Lord come into my house and stay." Her "first love" might have been quenched if they had refused. Her home became a center for the use of the church planting team. Verse 40 suggests that the church met in her home (Acts 16:15,40).

For Lydia an open home meant work and expense. Entertaining four men who would attract many others for counseling is a job. It probably meant embarrassment when the courts threw Paul and Silas into jail. Her commitment to hospitality was no small thing to her personal reputation, but more importantly it was a big boost to the growth of the new church. Hospitality is a necessary gift in an energetic young church that wants to grow.

The "place of prayer" by the river Gangites continued to be the daily evangelistic preaching point for the four men. On their way there they were often annoyed by a fortune teller, a slave girl possessed with an evil spirit associated with the Greek god Python.

She kept shouting after them that they were the "Servants of the Most High God proclaiming a way of salvation." It may be that Paul was upset at the subtle distortion of the truth in her use of the indefinite article "a," indicating that there were other ways of salvation. In any case the evangelists did not accept demonic testimony. Paul turned and exorcised the pythonic spirit from the girl (Acts 16:16-18).

Her owners were angry that her fortune telling powers were gone along with their own profits. They had Paul and Silas dragged before the magistrates in Philippi and mob pressure forced them to have the men beaten and thrown into prison and put into stocks (Acts 16:19-24).

A Jailor and His Household

The rest of the narrative is familiar to most. Paul and Silas were singing praises at midnight with many listening when suddenly an earthquake unfastened the stocks and opened the prison doors. The jailor was about to commit suicide when Paul shouted to him that none had escaped. Paul and Silas were brought outside and were amazed to hear the jailor asking, "Sirs, what must I do to be saved?" Paul told him, "Believe on the Lord Jesus Christ and you shall be saved, you and your household." Paul and Silas followed up by speaking "the word of the Lord to him together with all who were in his house." Evidently in the commotion his whole household had come. The jailor then "believed in God with his whole household," and immediately they were all baptized (Acts 16:25-34).[7] Growth was happening at Philippi.

PRINCIPLE: GOD USES NETWORKS OF PERSONAL RELATIONSHIPS TO BRING MANY TO HIMSELF

---

[7] It is often assumed that the jailor had infant children and this passage then becomes the authority for baptizing infants. All we know from the text is that they were old enough to "believe" (v. 34) and all who did were baptized (v. 33).

THE CHURCH IN PHILIPPI

The two conversion stories, which Luke the historian selected to mark the beginnings of the Philippian church have a common feature. In the cases of both Lydia and the jailor there is strong emphasis on the parallel conversion of their households. The household consisted of the extended family and the servants who also lived there. Lydia evidently brought her household to the riverside and they heard the Gospel and believed and were baptized (Acts 16:15). The jailor's household was specifically instructed to "believe" by Paul and we are told that they did believe (vv. 31,34). Then they were all baptized (v. 33).

Household relationships have tremendous evangelistic value. The already existing web of relationships in a household unit is a bridge to communicating the Gospel when one member becomes a Christian. This is what happened in the households of both Lydia and the jailor. They responded and their households followed them. An important decision is ever so much easier to make when a person you trust has already made it. The example they see carries more weight than logic or doctrinal argument.

Other passages in the New Testament illustrate this. When the apostle Peter went to Caesarea, he found that Cornelius had assembled his household so that they could all hear the Gospel (Acts 10:24). When Peter preached the forgiveness of sins through faith, the Holy Spirit fell on all who were listening (vv. 43,44). It was "household conversion." In the lifetime of Jesus, when the royal official arrived home to find that Jesus had healed his son, "He himself believed **and his whole household**" (John 4:53).

The principle of the household is not mystical, nor is it that there is some sort of grace which flows from the new convert to his extended family. It is simply that those closest to the new convert in a web of personal relationships are the most likely to join him in a life decision. The principle also works in less formal relationships such as friends, family members or business associates. Andrew found his brother Peter and brought him to Jesus (John 1:41). Philip found his friend Nathaniel (v. 45). (For an extended discussion see *The Master's Plan for Making Disciples*, by Win and Charles Arn, 1982, Church Growth Press.)

We cannot afford to overlook the application. Believers should be encouraged to strive for opportunities to witness among those within the relational networks of family, marketplace, neighborhood or association. New Christians especially have these networks containing unsaved friends and relatives. These are often the most "ripe" for the Gospel. The words of the Lord to the man recently delivered from possession by demons are appropriate for us. "Go home to your people and report to them what great things the Lord has done for you and how He had mercy on you" (Mark 5:19). "Your people" in this instruction is *oikos*, the word translated household in our Philippian connection. That is the place to begin in Christian witness.

The Church Which Loved Paul

Paul's initial stay in Philippi was shortened after the jail incident when the magistrates who released him and Silas from jail begged them to leave town. Paul, Silas and Timothy left going westward to Thessalonica while Luke evidently stayed in Philippi. The omission of the first personal pronoun "we" from Acts 16:16 until Acts 20:6, where Luke again includes himself as being in Philippi leads us to assume that Luke stayed there during the intervening years. Being a Gentile, Luke would not have the anti-Semitic disadvantage that Paul would have in a predominantly Roman city. His time there was no doubt spent in strengthening the church, although no record exists. We do know that the church there demonstrated its continued growth in the subsequent contacts with the Apostle.

The Philippians had developed a special love for Paul. It was demonstrated by the financial gifts they sent to him in Thessalonica and later in Corinth. He writes to the Philippians, "No church shared with me in the matter of giving and receiving, but you alone; for even in Thessalonica you sent a gift more than once for my needs. Not that I seek the gift itself, but I seek for the profit which increases to your account" (Phil. 4:15-17). Paul's response to their love is evident from his interest in their spiritual good as givers more than his temporal good as the receiver.

The love between Paul and the Philippians is the kind of love that exists between parent and child. Faithful caring church planters will strive for such a healthy relationship between themselves and the churches they establish. It is a growth stimulant because it keeps the vision of the new church in line with that of the planter. It also promotes open lines of communication for counsel and exhortation which may well be appropriate for the church's spiritual health.

The blessing of the bond between church planter and planted church brought Paul and the Philippian church together on a number of occasions after his initial visit. On his "third journey" he left Ephesus for Macedonia (Philippi) where he had occasion to give them much exhortation (Acts 20:1,2). It was then that he wrote Second Corinthians and boasted to them of the generosity he saw in the Philippian church (2 Cor. 8:1-5). He left to visit Corinth again but was back in Philippi within a few months (Acts 20:3-6). Still later, after Paul's imprisonments in Caesarea and Rome, he visited Philippi again from where he wrote First Timothy (1 Tim. 1:3). Our point in mentioning these details is simply to emphasize that Paul's bond with the church led to his repeated contacts with them which stimulated its growth.

Paul's epistles are an excellent example of continuing association with all the churches he planted. Tender plants need constant attention--feeding, weeding and watering. The epistle to the Philippians is perhaps the outstanding example of a church planter who finds tremendous pleasure in caring for the growing church. It radiates the warm relationship which existed between Paul and the Philippians, his "joy and crown" (Phil. 4:1).

Servant Leadership

Several features of Paul's strong bond with the Philippian church after he was forced to leave stand out in the letter he wrote to them. A look at these will give us some insights into similar situations in the 1990s. The first six verses are unique in their warmth.

Paul and Timothy, bondservants of Christ Jesus to all the saints in Christ Jesus who are in Philippi, including the overseers and deacons: Grace to you and peace from God our Father and the Lord Jesus Christ. I thank my God in all my remembrance of you. In view of your participation in the Gospel from the first day until now. For I am confident of this very thing, that He who began a good work in you will perfect it until the day of Christ Jesus (Phil. 1:1-6).

In the salutation Paul does not even mention his apostleship as in most of his writings, but labels himself only as a bondslave. The relationship between the church planter and the Philippian church was not based on Paul's apostolic authority over the church, but on Paul's willingness to be a slave of the Lord Jesus Christ in serving the church. The church found it a joy to respond to Paul's servant leadership. It was not necessary for him to "throw his weight around" when mutual love and respect existed. A slave has service to offer, not authority to impose.

Another feature of the relationship was the pleasure Paul found in thinking of them. And with every thought of them he praised God. Their "participation in the Gospel," from that "first day" when Lydia responded at the riverside, until the time of Paul's writing from prison in Rome, made Paul thankful and happy. As the Philippians experienced growth in the local church it literally thrilled the apostle.

A Church Planter's Prayer

A third feature of the relationship was Paul's consistent prayer for the growing church. Every time Paul thought of them he prayed for them--an attitude of prayer (Phil. 1:3). And we are left in no doubt as to how Paul prayed. The main features of his prayers for the Philippians are clear.

And this I pray, that your love may abound still more and more in real knowledge and all discernment. So that you may approve the things that are excellent, in order to be sincere and blameless

THE CHURCH IN PHILIPPI

until the day of Christ. Having been filled with the fruit of righteousness which comes through Jesus Christ to the glory and praise of God (Phil. 1:9-11).

Paul's prayer for the young church may surprise us. He did not pray for a larger audience or bigger building. He prayed that their love might abound. The New Testament church must be a place where people demonstrate the love of Christ. Genuine love will attract others. Note though, that he prayed for love that is consistent with the truth, not just sloppy emotion. And also that their love might be in all discernment, not just freebies for every outstretched hand.

A second request in the prayer was that they might learn to distinguish things that differ and choose excellence. We too live in a day when spiritual and moral excellence is sometimes compromised for the sake of the rhetorical or artistic talent. Paul's intercession focused on a pure and blameless church in Philippi. His third request was that the fruit of righteousness be exemplified among them. He prays that their actions might win praise for God, especially in the light of the coming "Day of Christ" (Phil. 1:10).

Thus the great church planter of the New Testament prays that their love might be discerning, that their choices might be morally excellent and that their actions might bring praise to God. We have a great deal to learn about the church planter's prayer life. We should study deeply the model prayers of the model church planter in Philippians, Ephesians and Colossians.

Striving For The Faith Of The Gospel

Following his great prayer Paul exhorts the believers in Philippi toward united spiritual progress in these important areas, all of which are vital to any growing church. In each of these he describes his own experience as an example for them to follow. The first exhortation is that they join together in defending the faith. Note the following phrases from chapter one which start with Paul's example and end with the instruction.

"My circumstances have turned out for the greater progress of the gospel.

I am appointed for the defense of the gospel.

I shall continue with you all for your progress in the faith.

Only conduct yourselves in a manner worthy of the Gospel of Christ.

So that....I may hear....that you are standing firm in one spirit, with one mind striving together for the faith of the gospel; in no way alarmed by your opponents.

Experiencing the same conflict which you saw in me and now hear to be in me (Phil. 1:12,17,25,27,28,30).

The thrust of these passages is that Paul in Rome was defending the gospel in the face of opposition. All he wanted was that Christ should be exalted and that the progress of the Philippian church be maintained (Phil. 1:20,25). In the light of his example he urges the Philippian believers to strive together for the faith. They too faced opposition and so Paul exhorts them to stand firm in unity to maintain the truth of the Gospel. They would have to suffer, but they could be encouraged by the example of Paul.

Churches with Biblical growth as a goal will face opposition against which they must stand firm. In the West opposition may come in the form of secular pressure, of lowering moral standards, or resistance from false religions. "Striving together for the faith of the Gospel" is not just a cliche for our preachers, but a description of the army of the Lord standing against the counsels of hell (Matt. 16:18).

Serving the Interests of Others

The second exhortation in the letter to the Philippians is that they serve together the interests of other people.

THE CHURCH IN PHILIPPI

Intent on one purpose. Do nothing from selfishness....but with humility of mind let each of you regard one another as more important than himself.

Do not merely look out for your own personal interests, but also for the interests of others.

Have this attitude in yourselves which was also in Christ Jesus.

I am being poured out as a drink offering upon the sacrifice and service of your faith (Phil. 2:2-5,17).

Here again there is both instruction and example. The instruction is that they be intent on one purpose--to make the interests of others come before personal interests. People in any church will respond positively when other believers take their interests seriously. The majority of Christians in a typical evangelical church are so concerned with promoting their selfish interests, that they only pay lip service to those things which interest others. It is no wonder that the attrition rate of visitors is so high.

Paul follows the instruction with four examples of the unselfish attitude which puts the interests of others first. Christ Jesus heads the list. He took the form of a servant and humbled Himself to the point of death on a cross (Phil. 2:5-8). Paul uses his own life as another example of selfless service. "I am being poured out as a drink offering upon the sacrifice and service of your faith (v. 17).

Timothy is the next example as one who was "Genuinely concerned for your welfare." Unlike the others, "who seek after their own interests" (Phil. 2:19-22). Epaphroditus was the last mentioned who put the interests of Paul above his own, acting as the servant of the Philippian church ministering to Paul in prison (vv. 25-30). All four of these are models for the believers in a growing church.

Attaining to the Knowledge of Christ

The third of the important exhortations associated with the healthy growth of the Philippian church is that they constantly press on toward the goal of maturity in Christ. Again Paul uses himself as an example. "Join in following my example."

> I count all things to be loss in view of the surpassing value of knowing Christ Jesus my Lord. That I may know Him, and the power of His resurrection...in order that I may attain to the resurrection from among the dead. Not that I have already obtained it or become perfect. I press on toward the goal for the prize of the upward call of God in Christ Jesus. Let us therefore as many as are perfect, have this attitude (Phil. 3:8,10,12,14,15).

As an insight into growing churches, the spiritual maturity of the believers is vital. Paul exhorts the Philippians to follow his example, and so they in turn are to be the examples to the new believers who are coming in to the fellowship. Two of the leading women were giving the wrong example because of a dispute. Paul urges them to end it and to live in harmony (Phil. 4:2,3). When Christ is their goal and prize, the bickering will end and the model of their Christlikeness will attract others.

So the story of the growing church in Philippi provides for us one of the great models on display in the New Testament with an emphasis on the power of love.

GROWTH INSIGHTS FROM PHILIPPI

1. Guidance for the location of pioneer
    evangelism   50
2. The advantage of cooperative team effort   52
3. Selecting a city for planting a church   53
4. Studying the soil before plowing   53
5. Church growth is a work of God   54
6. Hospitality builds churches   55
7. Accepting adversity with joy   56
8. Household networks for evangelism   57
9. Growing churches are loving churches   58
10. Growing churches are giving churches   59
11. Servant leadership, a must   59
12. A church planter's prayer   60
13. Striving for the faith of the Gospel   61
14. Serving the interests of others   62
15. Attaining to the knowledge of Christ   64

Chapter 4

THE CHURCH IN THESSALONICA
The Whole Truth
for Growth to Maturity

"Operation Thessalonica" is one of the most significant church planting efforts described in the New Testament. Its triple impact--on the city, on the believers and on the church--gives us an outstanding model to study. The city felt the effect of the Gospel which Paul described as coming "in power and in the Holy Spirit." The believers too were changed in terms of their lifestyle. They "became imitators of us and of the Lord." The church too was impacted by the power of the Gospel, and the change was observed by other believers in the whole province as well as the next province to the south. "You became an example to all the believers in Macedonia and Achaia" (1 Thess. 1:5,6,7).

Thessalonica commands a strategic position in the north-western corner of the Aegean Sea which has contributed to its continuing importance to the present time. It was not only a major port city with a fine harbor, it was on the intersection of two interstate highways of the Roman Empire in the first century. It was founded three hundred years before by one of Alexander's generals, Cassander, who named it after his wife. In the first century it had a population of around 200,000 including a large Jewish minority and was the capital of the Roman Province of Macedonia. For these reasons, it was politically, commercially and militarily important to Rome's interests. And for the same reasons it had strategic value for the interests of the Kingdom of God and locating a living church. Paul capitalized on them.

When Paul and his co-workers arrived in Thessalonica, their choice of that location was not the result of a panic decision because things were getting "hot" in Philippi. The narrative begins with the statement that Paul deliberately "passed" two other cities to get there, Amphipolis and Apollonia (Acts 17:1). The evangelists did not stop. Instead they continued on to Thessalonica. Apparently this was because there was a synagogue of the Jews there, specifically emphasized by Luke (v. 1).

> Now when they had travelled through Amphipolis and Apollonia, they came to Thessalonica, where there was a synagogue of the Jews. And according to Paul's custom, he went to them, and for three Sabbath days reasoned with them from the Scriptures, explaining and giving evidence that the Christ had to suffer and rise again from the dead and saying, "This Jesus whom I am proclaiming to you is the Christ." And some of them were persuaded and joined Paul and Silas, along with a great multitude of the God-fearing Greeks and a number of the leading women (Acts 17:1-4).

According to "his custom," Paul first went into the synagogue. He had done this before in the cities of Pisidian Antioch and at Iconium (Acts 13:14; 14:1). He could not follow this "custom" in Philippi where there was no synagogue, but only a handful of Jewish women meeting for prayer. He did it again in Berea (17:10), Athens (17:17), and Corinth (18:4). In this he emulated the Lord Jesus who began His public ministry in Nazareth using his privilege in the synagogue to preach the Good News. "As was his custom, he entered the synagogue on the Sabbath and stood up to read....." (Luke 4:16ff).

PRINCIPLE: THE CULTURAL CONTEXT PROVIDES AVENUES OF APPROACH FOR THE GOSPEL

In the study on the churches of Galatia we noted that synagogues provided the initial "target group" in Paul's master-plan for evangelism. Both godly Jews and the God-fearing Gentiles were found there. Thessalonica was no exception. So Paul put his plan into operation again. It had proved successful, though hazardous, so he continued to use it. The hazard of personal danger was only a minor factor in Paul's strategy. The major factor was that a living local church resulted from the strategy.

The principle Paul used was simply taking advantage of a cultural privilege he had to communicate to a target group he wanted to reach. This can be applied today in many ways. An expert at cross stitch might target the local cross stitch group for witness. She has an "in." A member of a lifeless denomination might use his/her privilege to teach a Sunday school class there. A converted substance abuser might work for God within community support groups where he/she has a voice. The possibilities are endless.

Paul's re-use of a workable strategy provides an insight for us in that he was not under compulsion to be constantly changing his approach. When he found a strategy which was blessed by God in a particular set of circumstances, he used it again in another city with a similar situation as he did in Thessalonica. Church planters today do not need to always have a new and novel approach. Nor do they need to use a new strategy just published in a Christian magazine. As the colloquial proverb says, "If it ain't broke, don't fix it." Use successful strategies as long as they result in the growth of healthy churches in the local cultural setting. Thoughtfully and prayerfully change them when they are no longer working, but don't change them for the sake of change.

A home Bible study strategy may work well in middle class suburbia, and should be repeated in another similar suburb. But it may not work so well in a farming community, or an ethnically mixed neighborhood. The Sunday school approach may produce results in a community of young families, but hardly in a yuppie community in Chicago's north shore. However what does work in a yuppie community may wisely be repeated in another.

The synagogue was the key to Pauline evangelistic strategy in the Roman world. However once he had gained entry, Paul used different techniques within the general strategy. Note, for instance that in the synagogues at Antioch and Iconium, Paul took the opportunity to preach in the oratorical mold (Acts 13:15ff; 14:1). The preaching was with such power that a great multitude believed (14:1).

The Approach Through Reason

However, in Thessalonica he took another approach, that of reasoning and argument. "He reasoned with them from the Scriptures, explaining and giving evidence that Christ had to suffer and rise again from the dead" (Acts 17:2,3). Paul had answers for their questions and rebuttals for their objections. He was a persuaded man persuading others through dialogue. He knew that his message was a fulfillment of the very Scriptures opened in the synagogue. For three sabbaths the warmth and logic of his arguments attracted the attention of many in the synagogue.

Reasoning as a method was valid, but the content of it was vital. Enough is known of Paul, Silas and Timothy to know the direction of their arguments. He had already written Galatians which is a reasoned treatise on the validity of the Gospel of the grace of God. No doubt his lines of argument to the Jews and God-fearers in Thessalonica would be similar. The authority of the Bible was his foundation. "He reasoned with them from the Scriptures" (Acts 17:2). No other foundation was stable. Argument after argument emerged from the open scroll of the Law and the Prophets as Paul pointed out the truth of God from them.

He also reasoned that the Lord Jesus Christ is the outstanding theme of revelation in the Scriptures. Note the phrases in the record, "Explaining and giving evidence that the Christ had to suffer and to rise again from the dead, and saying, 'This Jesus whom I am proclaiming to you is the Christ'" (Acts 17:3). Paul was patiently pointing out that the whole Old Testament (as we refer to it) is a prophetic history leading to Jesus of Nazareth who is the Messiah.

The Pharisees and many other Jews had failed to recognize Him because He came in humility as a servant and died on the cross. They had expected a powerful King. Paul showed that the Scriptures clearly

THE CHURCH IN THESSALONICA

foretold the sufferings of Messiah, "Christ had to suffer." He went on to show that, "Christ had .... to rise again." His resurrection was not only predicted, but was incontrovertible proof that He was the Messiah He claimed to be. So Paul's reasoning focused on the centrality of Christ in the Scriptures, the truth that Jesus of Nazareth was the Christ, and the importance of His death and resurrection.

Paul's approach through reason and the Scriptures is a good model for evangelistic home Bible studies today. Middle class Americans see homes as a non-competitive place to meet, no matter what their religious affiliation. The Bible itself is the authority and good leaders will insist on this. The subject must ultimately turn to the Lord himself, no matter what Bible book or truth is under consideration. True Bible study and true doctrine center on the Lord. All truth is related to Him and the Scriptures reveal "the things concerning Himself" (Luke 24:27). In these days there are some who want to concentrate on the experiential and the psychological. They tend to interpret Scripture by the way they "feel" about a passage. The wise leader will focus on the passage of Scripture and its plain teaching. If so, he/she will be pauline.

Decisions are Important

One further part of Paul's logic appears in our text. It is that Paul was asking people for a decision. "And some of them were persuaded and joined Paul and Silas" (Acts 17:4). The importance of a believing response to the truth of the Scripture was as vital then as it is today. Thus, Paul and Silas pressed them for a decision. Perhaps in the last couple of decades this word "decision" or "decision for Christ" has lost some of its punch because of being used in vague context. However, the fact remains that unless a hearer of the Word acts on it by personally receiving Christ, he/she remains outside the family of God.

Some of the Thessalonian Jews believed, including Jason who became host to the three missionaries (Acts 17:7); and probably also Aristarchus and Secundus (Acts 20:4). In addition to the Jews, a great multitude of the God-fearing Greeks and a few of the wives of leading families in the city, people of influence, believed. Because of the response to gospel persuasion their welcome ran out in the synagogue, so that the believers were forced to leave. They joined Paul and Silas who continued for an unspecified period, probably a few months, teaching and evangelizing while using the house of Jason as a center. The use of private homes for church activities should not be discounted in the strategies of modern churches. Home Bible studies is only one option which some churches are using successfully. The Cell group idea developed by Paul Cho in Seoul, Korea is another. One church has 18,000 cell groups operating within it!

After their departure from the synagogue, the focus of their evangelistic activity was turned toward another target group: idol-worshipping Gentiles. Paul's statement in his first letter not long after leaving Thessalonica says, "you turned to God from idols to serve a living and true God" (1 Thess. 1:9). It indicates that probably the majority of believers in the church had been pagan until the evangelists arrived with the Gospel. When one door is shut, try another.

It's Dynamite

The powerful preaching of the Good News is an outstanding feature of its presentation to Thessalonica. It touched well-versed Jews and unversed pagans. It reached leading ladies of the city who no doubt had considerable influence on others. It also reached the thinking Gentiles who were disgusted with the immoral idol worship of Greek and Roman gods. Small wonder that Paul wrote to the Romans a few years later that the Gospel was the "power of God for salvation for everyone who believes, to the Jew first and also to the Greek" (Rom. 1:16). Power is the word from which we get the English word "dynamite."

It is quite understandable that his opponents in Thessalonica accused him of "turning the world upside down" (Acts 17:6 KJV). Although technically these words were a legal accusation that the evangelists were disturbing the peace, it is also true that the power of the Gospel can turn a community "upside down." And Paul was correct when he said in his first

THE CHURCH IN THESSALONICA

letter to them a few weeks later, "Our gospel did not come to you in word only, but also in power and in the Holy Spirit and with full conviction" (1 Thess. 1:5). The topsy-turvy world of the Thessalonians needed to be turned over by a mighty work of God.

Tough Opposition

Opposition had been part of the church growth story there from the beginning. Paul reminded them of that in his first letter, "As you know we had the boldness in our God to speak to you amid much opposition" (1 Thess. 2:2). As more and more people came to Christ the displeasure of Satan became increasingly evident. The "much opposition" reached crisis proportions. The young church suddenly faced an angry mob, a jealous synagogue and some very concerned civil officials. This is the record.

> But the Jews becoming jealous and taking along some wicked men from the market place, formed a mob and set the city in an uproar; coming upon the house of Jason they were seeking to bring them out to the people. And when they did not find them, they began dragging Jason and some brethren before the city authorities, shouting, "These men who have upset the world have come here also. And Jason has welcomed them and they all act contrary to the decrees of Caesar, saying that there is another king, Jesus." And they stirred up the crowd and the city authorities who heard these things. And when they had received a pledge from Jason and the others, they released them. And the brethren immediately sent Paul and Silas away by night (Acts 17:5-10).

External reasons for the church coming under fire are not hard to find. The synagogue leaders would certainly be jealous when people were leaving to follow Jesus the Messiah whom they themselves had rejected. The husbands of the "leading women" who had been saved could easily be persuaded to question the motives of the evangelists from out of town. To them, their motives might include money and lust. Paul seems to refer to this when he wrote in the context of opposition to the Gospel. "Our exhortation does not come from...impurity or by way of deceit" (1 Thess 2:2,3). These men would be slow to understand theological distinctions and quick to look for sensual motives.

Also, the Roman officials were no doubt already nervous about the new religion called Christianity, which they perceived to be a Jewish sect. The city officials of Thessalonica knew that there was widespread unrest in the Jewish communities of the Empire, especially in Judea. Claudius Caesar had recently expelled all the Jews from Rome for that reason (Acts 18:2). He had called them "a general plague throughout the whole world." So from the Roman point of view this Jewish sect needed careful watching.

No doubt Satan provided the inspiration to the Synagogue officials as they cleverly combined all of these factors to effect the ouster of Paul and his team. Their plan worked well. They rounded up some riffraff from the market place and paid them to start a riot which would gain the ears of the city officials and the leading citizens. Not finding Paul and Silas at Jason's house, they dragged Jason and some other believers to a city court. They accused him and the evangelists of sedition and of proclaiming a rival to Caesar, a king named Jesus. Sedition was a serious charge in the context of the Roman world. The result was that the magistrate forced Jason to put up a bail bond insuring that Paul would quickly and quietly leave town and not come back.

Behind the Opposition--Satan

Growing churches today will also face opposition from the same enemy. It is for this reason that we have reviewed the enemy's attack on the Thessalonian church. The same enemy is still inspiring willing agencies to defame Christian leaders, to cast suspicion on their moral conduct and to use a willing media to publicize it. The insatiable public greed for character defamation makes the task relatively easy. Evangelicals who are faithful to the Word are often accused of narrow-mindedness because we preach salvation by

THE CHURCH IN THESSALONICA 75

grace through faith in Christ Jesus. We are tagged with a sexist label because of the Biblical roles for Christian men and women. We are viciously attacked if we suggest Biblical righteousness should be practiced in society on issues such as abortion, euthanasia and "gay rights." The attacks will not go away, but the true Church must continue to flourish in a world just as corrupt as that of the first century.

In Thessalonica Satan seemed to have the upper hand. The fledgling church was on the defensive and the missionaries were forced to leave. Without them it faced further ridicule as an orphan with runaway parents. The props were suddenly gone. Would it survive without their strength and support? The answer was, "yes, it would survive," though the pressure of persecution continued.

Encouragement Through Return Visits

In the following months, Paul was hindered from going back because of the price on Jason's head, but this did not stop him from trying, though he felt the opposition of Satan. In his first letter to them Paul told of his efforts to visit, but "Satan thwarted us" (1 Thess. 2:18). Then when he "could endure it no longer" he sent Timothy to strengthen and encourage them in the faith (2 Thess. 3:2). Again he wrote, "When I could endure it no longer, I also sent to find out about your faith, for fear that the tempter might have tempted you" (v. 5). Like a parent unwillingly separated from his children, Paul tried everything he knew to get back to the Thessalonians. Eventually his efforts were rewarded.

The church was started during what we call his "Second Missionary Journey." On this journey he went as far west as Corinth, from where Paul returned to Antioch by ship without retracing his steps through Thessalonica. On his third journey he travelled overland to Ephesus and spent almost three years there after which he went to Macedonia. It was then that he almost certainly visited Thessalonica for Luke says, "He had visited those districts" (Acts 20:2). He went on to Corinth again from where he began collecting money for the poor in Jerusalem.

His third visit to Thessalonica was in connection with the collection for the Jerusalem believers. From Corinth he retraced his steps around the Aegean Sea visiting all the churches for this purpose. Each church chose couriers to carry the money and accompany him to Jerusalem. Among the contributing churches was Thessalonica and the couriers selected from there were Aristarchus and Secundus (Acts 20:4). Nothing else of that visit is recorded, but it can be assumed that Paul used that opportunity to the fullest extent possible.

His fourth and final visit to this church was between his two imprisonments in Rome. We have no specific statements, but a perusal of the following passages indicates that he did go to Macedonia at that time, and no doubt included a visit to the church in Thessalonica, Paul's "joy and crown" (Phil. 1:25,26; 2:24; 1 Tim. 1:3; 2 Tim. 4:3).

Accountability--A Growth Factor

The principle of repeated visits by the spiritual parent of the church is a definite growth factor. The fact that the parent leaves the church after it is established gives the young church a chance to mature, as we noted in Galatia. The fact that he comes back reinforces the young church's sense of identity and belonging with the founder. The knowledge that he is coming makes them accountable for the principles of Christian life and community he has previously taught them. So the result is that the quality of the fellowship is enhanced. The accountability of the church to the spiritual parent is a powerful incentive toward positive change, and no one has more influence for this change than the parent.

Role Model For The Young Church

The first letter to the Thessalonians reveals some instructive insights into the growth of the local church. One of these stems from Paul's defense of his personal character. Timothy had returned from his visit with the report that the Jews in the city were making personal attacks on him in order to shake the faith of his converts. It was pure slander. So Paul countered the

THE CHURCH IN THESSALONICA

charges by asking the believers to think back to his life and character during the months he was living among them. This is what he wrote.

> You know what kind of men we proved to be among you for your sake. You also became imitators of us and of the Lord...For our exhortation does not come from error or from impurity or by way of deceit; but just as we have been approved by God to be entrusted with the gospel, so we speak, not as pleasing men but God, who examines our hearts...For we never came with flattering speech, as you know, nor with a pretext for greed--God is witness. Nor did we seek glory from men...But we proved to be gentle among you, as a nursing mother tenderly cares for her own children. Having thus a fond affection for you, we were well pleased to impart to you, not only the gospel, but also our own lives, because you had become very dear to us...You are witnesses, and so is God, how devoutly and uprightly and blamelessly we behaved toward you believers, just as you know how we were exhorting and encouraging and imploring each of you as a father would his own children (1 Thess. 1:5,6; 2:3-11).

The length of this quote is justified because of what it reveals of Paul's character as a church planter in Thessalonica. His ministry among them had been far more than words; it was a ministry of character. The truth of his words was fully demonstrated, and could be proved, by the integrity of his life. So to refute the slander of his enemies, Paul asks them simply to ponder his character which they knew well. Probably nothing is more crucial to the planter of a local church than that his life be consistent with his speech.

Paul reminds them that the lives of Silas, Timothy and himself had "proved" what kind of men they were. So much so that the Thessalonian believers had used them as "role models." Paul stated that they became "imitators of us." That was a compliment to the consistent lives of the missionaries. There is a distinction to be made between a "role model" which should be followed and a cult leader whose "hold" on his followers is psychological rather than exemplary. Cult leaders often get people to implicitly obey their every whim while their lives are deceitful and immoral. Paul states to those who knew him, "Our exhortation does not come from impurity or by way of deceit."

These verses give us other insights into the character of Paul's team as effective church growth leaders. Their goal was not to please man, but God. Happy people in the pews took second place to a well pleased God in heaven (1 Thess. 2:4,5). They called on God as the "examiner" of their hearts and as "witness" to their speech and desires because their success was not so much the measure of numbers but the pleasure of God.

Their care and handling of the new babes in Christ was compared to the gentleness of a nursing mother tenderly caring for her children (1 Thess. 2:7). Their love was proved by their selfless involvement for the sake of the believers. They poured their very lives into the growth of the church (v. 8). They asked no return of the Thessalonians, but with "labor and hardship" they worked "night and day" so as not to be a burden to any of them (v. 9). They worked in the role of a wise father instructing, encouraging and pleading with his children: "So that you may walk in a manner worthy of the God who calls you into His own kingdom and glory" (v. 12). The goal of the church planters for the Thessalonians was that their growth in Christ be marked by a lifestyle worthy of the kingdom and glory of God.

Doctrine For Church Growth

A remarkable feature in the growth process of the Thessalonian church is that it was stimulated by solid doctrine. The three man team of church planters was only there for a few months at most, yet they presented a broad spectrum of truth which some church growth specialists would consider unhealthy for a new church in a new locality. Less than a year elapsed from the first announcement of the gospel in that city and the establishment of a church there, to the completion of both of Paul's letters to them which we call First

THE CHURCH IN THESSALONICA   79

and Second Thessalonians. Remarkably these two letters indicate that the teaching which had been committed to the believers was not just the "milk of the Word," but "strong meat." Paul reminds them, "We kept telling you..."; "You know what commandments we gave you"; "Do you not remember that while I was still with you I was telling you these things" (1 Thess. 3:4; 4:2; 2 Thess. 2:5).

The foundational truths of the Gospel had been faithfully taught. The authority of Scripture, the promise of a Messiah who would both suffer an atoning death and rise again, the identity of Messiah with Jesus of Nazareth: all this had been proclaimed. They were also taught that genuine faith in Christ would be accompanied by turning away from their old lifestyle based on idolatry and by actively serving the living God (1 Thess. 1:10). Their faith, love and hope were to be active rather than passive, to which they responded (v. 3). These things were basic.

Their Christian experience was to be much more than enjoying entertaining services. They needed, and received, a solid foundation of Truth. They should have, and did, respond by actively repudiating their pagan past and just as actively promoting their new found faith.

The Whole Counsel Of God

Silas, Paul and Timothy were not content to merely bring them up to this "short flight cruising altitude" of truth and "level off." Even in those first weeks, they continued on up to the "stratosphere" of truth so the Thessalonian believers could view the "whole counsel of God." In these two epistles Paul casually refers to many theological truths with which his readers were already familiar. They were acquainted with the truth of election (1 Thess. 1:4; 2:12), the Fatherhood of God (1:4), the personality of the Holy Spirit (1:5), the reality of Satan (2:18), etc. They had been taught to expect the coming of the Lord Jesus Christ for His church (1:10), the coming judgment in the Day of the Lord (5:2-4), the wrath of God (5:9), and the coming of the "man of lawlessness" (2 Thess 2:3-5).

We should not miss the significance of all this. New

believers, hungry for the Word of God, were not denied the full spectrum of teachings. As Paul said to the Ephesians, "I did not shrink from declaring to you the whole purpose of God" (Acts 20:27). Many church leaders today avoid certain subjects like prophecy, judgment, and the Holy Spirit as being "divisive," or only for older believers. Those who take this position find support by the argument of Paul to the Corinthians that he had given them "milk" because they were not able to receive "solid food" (1 Cor. 3:2,3). However, it should be pointed out that the reason the Corinthians could not take "solid food" was not that they were young in Christ, but because they were carnal, allowing jealousy, strife and division among them (vv. 1,4).

Believers recently saved are often like hungry athletes at a good supper. They swallow truth by faith as fast as they can grasp it with their minds. Solid Biblical preaching and teaching is a primary growth factor. Every growing church needs a balanced "diet" of solid food. Note the word "balanced," but don't forget the solid food. So much of our modern church growth thinking comes with the emphasis on "taste" rather than on "nutrition." Leaders tend to be like some frustrated parents who give in to the infantile cries for "spiritual sugar pops" instead of insisting on the less tasty but more nutritious cereals for the long-term growth of strong believers in healthy churches.

The Lord called us to "make disciples" which is a great deal more than simply seeing people born into the family of God. It is bringing spiritual babes into maturity, by providing what is good for them, rather than what they think they want. The Thessalonian church grew on solid spiritual food. Don't settle for "sugar pops."

THE CHURCH IN THESSALONICA 81

GROWTH INSIGHTS FROM THESSALONICA

1. Strategic location selection   67
2. Planning for a strong initial thrust   68
3. The approach through reason and argument   70
4. Content for the reasoned approach   70
5. Decisions are important   71
6. The Gospel is dynamite   72
7. The strength of the opposition   73
8. Satan, the source of opposition   74
9. The church planter returns   75
10. Accountability of the church to the founder   76
11. The role model for a young church   76
12. The whole truth for the growing church   78
13. Scripture, the key to growth in Berea   79

Chapter 5

THE CHURCH IN CORINTH
Church Growth and the
Principle of Morality

The church at Corinth was established in the most hostile church planting environment of the first century. The spiritual atmosphere was poisoned by moral pollution. Idolatry contaminated the "living water" and the spiritual soil was hardened by greed for material things. Yet, in that very environment a healthy local church was planted which became the prize plant of Paul's "church garden" in Achaia (Acts 15:40--18:22). At the start it did not look promising.

Paul arrived in Corinth a discouraged man. Three churches had been planted in the province of Macedonia to the north, but in all three Paul had been forced to leave prematurely by commercial or religious interests. He had only recently escaped from Berea leaving Timothy and Silas (Acts 17:15). He went south to the Achaian city of Athens where Timothy had planned to meet him. While waiting there he became overwhelmed with the extreme idolatry of the city. He tried to reason with the Jews in the synagogue as well as the God-fearing gentiles. He even argued with the pagan in the market place. There was little response (vv. 16,17).

The philosophers called him an idle babbler because he spoke of Jesus and the resurrection. However, they did give him an opportunity to explain his message to their council. They listened to him until he mentioned the resurrection at which point they began to sneer (Acts 17:19-32). The total result at Athens was that some few men and an undistinguished woman named Damaris believed (v. 34). Compared to the results in the Macedonian cities Athens was disappointing. Paul's discouragement level rose further without the companionship of Timothy and Silas.

Lonely, Discouraged and Broke

Alone, Paul left Athens and travelled forty miles west to Corinth. He himself described his condition at the time, "in weakness, in much fear and trembling" (1 Cor. 2:3). It was probably early in the summer of 51 A.D. Physically and emotionally Paul was drained after a strenuous year of travel and evangelism. Athens had been a disappointment. He seems also to have been in financial need for the first thing he did in Corinth was to find employment. In short he was lonely, discouraged and broke.

Corinth was a leading city in the Empire. It enjoyed a strategic location astride a narrow isthmus which joined mainland Greece with the southern peninsula. It had seaports on both the Adriatic and the Aegean seas which made it a major trading center of the Mediterranean world. Lavish theaters and palaces displayed the commercial prosperity, but Corinth was probably best known for its moral degradation. To "play the Corinthian" was a Roman proverb for sexual laxity. The temple of Aphrodite which crowned the fortified hill above the city employed a thousand female slaves as prostitutes in the veneration of the goddess. Corinth in Roman times was said to be the most wicked city since Sodom and Gomorrah.

Temples to other pagan deities such as Melcertes and Apollo added to the idolatrous character of the city. Paul did not arrive with his eyes closed. When he later wrote to the Christians there he complained that the city paid respect to "many gods and many lords" (1 Cor. 8:5). Poseidon, the sea god, was the patron deity of the famous Isthmian Games held in Corinth every two years. As in Athens, idol gods were literally everywhere. Could the church of the living God take root and grow in a place like that?

Tentmaking

Paul's first need was to find accommodation and employment. He obtained both when he found Aquila, a Jew who owned a tent-making business. Aquila and his wife Priscilla had recently come from Rome because the emperor Claudius had issued an edict expelling Jews from the capital. They had set up their business in Corinth when Paul found them and worked with them. They gave Paul a job and took him into their home. Paul had learned tentmaking as a boy and now put it to use as gainful employment. In all probability Aquila and Priscilla were already believers when Paul met them. They became Paul's life-long friends and among his most loyal helpers in church planting. When Paul wrote to the Roman Christians he told them that all the churches of the Gentiles owed thanks to Priscilla and Aquila (Rom. 16:4).

A valuable insight emerges from Paul's secular work in Corinth: that sometimes it is both necessary and advantageous for a church planter to use his skills in the market place so as not to be dependent on the infant church. Paul had worked before while planting the church in Thessalonica. He wrote to them from Corinth reminding them that "working night and day so as not to be a burden to any of you, we proclaimed to you the Gospel of God" (1 Thess 2:9). He did it again in Ephesus. "These hands ministered to my own needs and to the men who were with me" (Acts 20:34).

Paul did not consider it beneath his dignity to work in a secular setting when the circumstance made it more effective for the Gospel. He wanted to demonstrate the normal means by which most Christian believers meet life's material needs: by secular employment. This does not negate the general principle that those who "proclaim the Gospel...get their living from the Gospel" (1 Cor. 9:14). However it does highlight another principle that the servant of God may not always demand his rights to remuneration. Paul referred to this principle when writing to the Corinthians later, "We did not use this right, but we endure all things that we may cause no hindrance to the Gospel of Christ" (v. 12).

Several times in the beginning of a new work Paul found it expedient to support himself. His practice is still valid and used today by thousands of evangelical church planters all over the world. Not only is it sound Biblical practice, it also dispels an all-too-common idea that evangelists are lazy. Twice in the New Testament Paul refers to his secular work to support the genuineness of his motives (1 Thess 2:9; Acts 20:34). Corinth was a predominantly commercial city so Paul demonstrated that the Good News was not commercial. He has left us an excellent model, especially in a Christian world where all too often the bottom line is "how much does it pay"?

Preaching Christ Crucified

As usual, Paul made the synagogue his first point of contact trying to persuade both Jews and Greeks that Jesus was the promised Messiah of the Scriptures. One of the early manuscripts says that he inserted the Name of the Lord Jesus at appropriate points in the Scripture readings. After a few Sabbaths Timothy and Silas arrived with good news from Berea, and Paul seems to have been greatly encouraged by their report so that he began concentrating his whole being on the proclamation of the Gospel. "Devoting himself completely to the word, solemnly testifying to the Jews that Jesus was the Christ" (Acts 18:5).

Reaction to the increased intensity of Paul's arguments was not long in coming. Some were persuaded, but the majority resisted his arguments and blasphemed the Lord Jesus. At this point Paul used the words of Ezekiel about the faithful watchman who warned the house of Israel though they would not listen. "Your blood be upon your own heads, I am clean; from now on I shall go to the Gentiles" (Acts 18:6; Ezek. 33:1-9). His responsibility as a messenger was to clearly present the message. If they rejected the message then Paul demonstrated that he was absolved from responsibility.

There is an important insight here for the evangelist. Having clearly and fully presented the Gospel Paul pressed for a decision which effectively divided the non-believers from the believers. No sweet talk, no avoiding of the issues and no assumption that because they believed the Jewish Scriptures they were at least halfway in the door of faith. Instead an earnest pressing of the claims of Christ on his hearers. His message to Corinth was not an impressive presentation, but simply "Jesus Christ and Him crucified" (1 Cor. 2:2). The cross demands a decision from those who consider it at all. It is either an offense or it is the only hope for salvation.

There could be no compromising the message to

avoid offending some hearers. Paul spoke of the "offense of the cross" (Gal. 5:11) knowing that it was a stumbling block to the Jews and foolishness to the Gentiles (1 Cor. 1:23). The cross implies that man has no moral basis on which he can meet God so it is offensive to any but true believers.

PRINCIPLE: MORAL ISSUES ARE VITAL TO THE HEALTH OF GROWING CHURCHES

A common error today is to consciously avoid offending anyone so they will keep attending the church services. The attendance chart is thought to reveal the success of the church rather than the reality of the people's faith. Because the cross deals with the issues of God's holiness and man's sinfulness it acts as a tester of true faith. Paul did not shrink from bringing his audience to the point of decision with the full implications of the cross in view. When the rejecters used abusive and blasphemous language about the crucified Christ he protested by shaking out his clothing and leaving the synagogue. He said that he would concentrate on preaching to the Gentiles since they would not listen. Morality is non-negotiable for Biblical church growth.

The Nucleus Of The Young Church

The intensity of Paul's preaching of the Word and the definite break with Jewish opposition resulted in some key converts right at the start. The first mentioned is Titius Justus, a Gentile who had been a worshipper of God in the synagogue and now became a believer in Jesus Christ as Savior. His house, next to the synagogue, became the meeting place for the first Christians there. He is probably identical with Gaius in Romans 16:23 and his full name was Gaius Titius Justus. His warm hospitality to believers was such that Paul describes him as "host to me and to the whole church." He was one of the first converts baptized in Corinth (1 Cor. 1:14).

Another who was an early convert baptized by Paul was Crispus, a superintendent of the synagogue. His conversion was followed by that of his household relatives and servants (Acts 18:8; 1 Cor. 1:14). A third convert in the initial nucleus was Stephanus, not mentioned in Acts, but in a letter to Corinth about those who Paul had baptized (1 Cor. 1:16). Stephanas and his household also came in for special mention in the salutation of the letter. Paul called them the "firstfruits of Achaia" because they were the earliest believers.

They had "devoted themselves for ministry to the saints" by unselfishly serving others in the local church (1 Cor. 16:15). Families like that of Stephanas are invaluable to young churches in two ways. Their willingness to meet needs is always in demand and the ministry model they provide to newer believers encourages them to get involved too. The energy potential of young churches increases enormously with families like that of Stephanas. Pity the church where the hottest people are those warming pews.

Just a Number--Tertius

The nucleus continued to grow. There was a man named Erastus who was city treasurer (Rom. 16:23). And a woman named Chloe who reported on some of the divisions (1 Cor. 1:11). Two other interesting people were Tertius and Quartus, literally *third* and *fourth* (Rom. 16:22,23). "Third" was Paul's secretary to whom he dictated the letter to the Romans and "Fourth" is simply described as "the brother.". Number-names usually indicated slaves or former slaves who were given numbers in the order of their purchase. These two were probably people who were insignificant in society, but they come in for special mention in the church context. They represent thousands of God's choice ones in churches today who are just **numbers** in the society of this world. But they are the elite in the kingdom of God and the very backbone of growing churches. Tertius represents many like him who are humble enough to be known as just a number in their service for God and His church. We used to sing a Sunday School chorus which emphasizes the character of Paul's secretary, Third.

I come third, I come third,
Where God puts me in His Word.
God is first, and others second,--I come third.
  Author unknown

Discouragement and Fear

Many Corinthians heard the Word, believed and were baptized (Acts 18:8). It was a remarkable beginning, but it was taking a toll on the Apostle. The heavy responsibilities were weighing on him as they do on so many of God's servants who dare to invade "enemy territory." Depression crept in which accentuated his fears, real or imagined. Later Paul admitted these in his first letter, that he was with them "in weakness and in fear and in much trembling" (1 Cor. 2:3).

He had clashed with the Jews in the synagogue when they blasphemed the Lord Jesus. He was, no doubt, tired from strenuous labor and travel. Tentmaking full time plus a heavy schedule of preaching, debating and shepherding pushed his physical capacity to the limit. Added to this was the emotional impact of the city's depraved morals on him. About then he heard of a plot to have him indicted in court and run out of town. All these kinds of opposition had happened before, but the cumulative effect was "getting to him." Discouragement settled in as he became obsessed with the circumstances in Corinth. He was afraid (Acts 18:9).

Then the Lord acted in a remarkable way to encourage Paul by speaking to him in a night vision (Acts 18:9,10). Paul needed two things which God graciously provided: a fresh vision of Christ and a new assurance from the Word. These are the answer to the pressure of discouragement from tough circumstances. We are too often like the disciples in the storm on Galilee. They almost missed the presence of the Lord because they were concentrating on the wind and waves. It all changed when they heard Him say, "It is I" (John 6:20). To see Him and to hear Him changes everything. God seldom gives visions to us like that of Paul, but we have the advantage for we possess a fuller portrait of Christ and more of His Word than even Paul knew. Encouragement waits for all of us there to see and hear Him.

The encouraging word which Paul heard in the night had five parts to it (Acts 18:9,10). The first two were concerned with Paul's reaction to the circumstances. He was fearful and he wanted to quit preaching. The Lord's word was "don't fear and don't quit." The central one of the five words of encouragement was, "I am with you." It is the most often repeated promise in the Bible. God knows how often we need to be reminded. The final two were concerned with God's control over the circumstances and with His sovereign plan for the Corinthian church. "No one will...harm you for I have many people in this city." Church planters should often meditate on this passage.

> Fear not I am with thee; O be not dismayed!
> For I am thy God and will still give thee aid;
> I'll strengthen thee, help thee and cause thee to stand
> Upheld by My righteous, omnipotent hand (Isa. 41:10).

The vision and the voice of Christ had the designed effect on Paul. He overcame his fears, settled down for the next year and a half and faithfully taught the Word of God to the believers in the growing church. God silenced the Jewish opposition by sending to Corinth a governor (proconsul) named Gallio. Unlike the governors in Philippi and Thessalonica, Gallio was wise enough to discern that the charge of the Jews was religious and not under the jurisdiction of civil law, so he drove them away from the judgment seat. Case dismissed! In fact it backfired. The Jewish leader for the prosecution, Sosthenes, was seized by some Greeks in the court area and beaten. Gallio paid no attention (Acts 18:12-17). In the end God further encouraged the Apostle because Sosthenes himself became a believer and an associate of Paul (1 Cor. 1:1). Paul then stayed in Corinth for the next eighteen months building up the believers through his teaching. During these months Paul describes his ministry in two ways, in terms of a farmer planting seed and nurturing the plants in a field and in terms of a builder laying a foundation and building on it. These concepts were discussed in the introduction.

Paul Planted, Apollos Watered

Eighteen months of discipling and teaching soon passed during which time the church had progressed far enough to allow Paul to leave. The Corinthians had every spiritual gift in evidence (1 Cor. 1:5). With Priscilla and Aquila Paul left Corinth sailing from Cenchrea across the Aegean Sea to Ephesus, leaving Priscilla and Aquila to begin Christian work there.

During this time Apollos arrived in Ephesus from Alexandria, a well educated and highly talented man. Priscilla and Aquila were able to help him come to a full knowledge of Christ. Apollos then went on to Corinth where he arrived with a letter of introduction from the brethren in Ephesus (Acts 18:24-27).

Once in Corinth Apollos joined with the Christians there and debated with the Jews. "He powerfully refuted the Jews in public, demonstrating by the Scriptures that Jesus was the Christ" (Acts 18:28). The Corinthian Christians were impressed by his ability and many of them began calling themselves the disciples of Apollos. Perhaps his eloquence was superior to Paul's. It was not long before others who remembered Paul as their spiritual father formed a group emphasizing their loyalty to him. Their watchword was "I belong to Paul" (1 Cor. 1:12; 3:4). Party spirit was invading the church in Corinth.

The Danger of Cliques

The party spirit in Corinth did not come from Paul or Apollos. It came from group favoritism within the church. Paul only speaks in positive terms about Apollos in his writings and even urged Apollos to go back to Corinth (1 Cor. 16:12). The problem was with the church, not the evangelists.

Another party arose around the name of Peter. Some scholars suggest that Peter visited Corinth on his way to Rome with the result that a group rallied around his name. We don't know. Certainly Paul singles out Peter from the other apostles for special mention in First Corinthians (1 Cor.9:5; 15:5). Even if Peter did not visit Corinth, someone had strongly influenced the Corinthian Christians in Peter's name, perhaps pressing for the decision of the Jerusalem Council about food offered to idols to be applied in Corinth (Acts 15:29). Peter's credentials were unquestioned, but when a group within the church said "I am of Peter" it was divisive.

A fourth group emerged to complicate the picture. Perhaps in reaction to the other three groups there were those who said, "I am of Christ." Paul clearly indicated that their spiritual sounding claims were just as divisive as the other groups. His rhetorical question, "Has Christ been divided?," condemns them even more than the others (1 Cor. 1:13).

Party spirit is a growth stopper in many otherwise fine churches. It may develop around people, as it did in Corinth, or around issues such as getting involved in abortion demonstrations or campaigning for the exclusive use of the King James Bible. There always seems to be some dear saint with a pet project or peeve who spends his/her time drumming up a "party" to advance it or kill it. It is almost a given that they will encounter newcomers with their pet issue with the equally certain result that the newcomer is "turned off."

Dealing With Divisions

Party spirit has explosive capability for disaster in the church. When Paul received information in a letter from Chloe that these parties had formed and were already quarreling he wrote in strong language to correct it (1 Cor 1:10--4:21). He told them not to rest their faith on the attractiveness of man's wisdom, but on the power of God which was demonstrated at the cross. The cross left no room for boasting except in the Lord Himself (1:10-31).

He went on to say that God reveals His truth by His Spirit only to spiritual people. The strife and divisions among the Corinthian believers demonstrated that they were spiritual babies, carnal in their thinking (1 Cor. 3:1-3). It was God, not Paul, Apollos or Peter, who caused growth (vv. 4-20). Therefore it was wrong that they should boast of these leaders (v. 21). Paul asked that even he, as the founder of the church, be regarded merely as a servant of Christ and a trustee of God's truth (4:1-3). The Christians were to imitate Paul's servanthood and this left no room for pride in leaders (vv. 6,18).

Church leaders need to be alert for any divisive party spirit in a young church. Like the Corinthians, immature Christians tend to be influenced by leaders with charisma and to link their faith to them. Leaders sometimes fail to recognize the danger because of the subtle satisfaction it brings them. If they are wise they will realize that strong churches are based on the one Foundation and not on even the best of human leaders.

One Holy Church He Blesses

Seven chapters of Paul's first letter to the church in Corinth deal with the need for practical holiness in the church fellowship (1 Cor. 5--11). Cultural norms in the community are usually reflected in the church being planted there. When the norms are Biblically unacceptable the church must act to correct them. Corinth had a deserved reputation for moral degradation in the Roman world. Paul gave specific instructions about how to deal with these kinds of problems which still plague churches in that kind of culture. Compromising the standards of God for His holy church is a perpetual danger. There will always be a tension between the purity of the church and the size of the church.

The sanctity of the church in Corinth had been compromised by tolerating an immoral relationship. They even boasted about it as part of their liberty in Christ (1 Cor. 5). Paul instructed them in no uncertain terms to remove the offender (v. 2), "clean out the old leaven" (v. 7), "remove the wicked man from among yourselves" (v. 13). Historically known as excommunication, it is all too rarely practiced in evangelical churches today. The church in Corinth did as Paul instructed and the church was blessed (2 Cor. 2:6-11). Church growth must never compromise church sanctity. Unfortunately most church growth literature does not touch this subject.

Every form of discipline, from admonition to excommunication should have restoration as its goal, not separation. It should be practiced only by spiritual leaders with deep love and fervent prayer. The restored member of the local body will actually help its healthy growth by being a model and counsellor to others who may be in danger of falling where he/she fell. In the whole process the church will be strengthened.

The issue of morality in the church concerns the sanctity of the physical body which is the temple of the Holy Spirit (1 Cor. 6:12-20). The believer must never violate its sanctity by sexual immorality, but rather glorify God with his/her body. The sanctity of marriage and the family is vital to a church's health. The principle for the church was that each man have his own wife and each woman have her own husband (1 Cor. 7).

Another negative growth factor was that the Corinthian church had compromised the sanctity of their church as a fellowship of believers. Disputes between believers, instead of being handled within the fellowship, were being taken to secular courts. Three times Paul challenges this by reminding them of the God-given responsibility of believers to judge "matters of this life." The church, not the heathen judges, should settle these (1 Cor. 6:1-11). I need not expand on the contemporary church situation in North America where the church is mired in public litigation and splattered by the media because of it.

The First Corinthian letter was written while Paul was in Ephesus. The church evidently responded well to it. The moral issues were dealt with and litigation among Christians seems to have stopped. However Jewish legalists arrived from Palestine and conditions deteriorated in Corinth making it necessary for Paul to visit Corinth a second time going from Ephesus and returning there (2 Cor.11:4,22; 2:1; 12:14). Later Paul was openly insulted at Corinth by an anti-Paul party spokesman. Following this Titus was sent to Corinth with a "severe letter" (2:4,9; 7:8,12), and agreed to meet Paul in Troas with their response. A riot hastened Paul's departure from Ephesus. At some point Paul suffered "affliction in Asia," perhaps in Troas (1:8-11). He crossed to Macedonia, where Titus met him with a report of a good response of the Corinthians to the "severe letter" (7:5-16). He continued evangelizing northward into Illyricum and upon returning to Macedonia heard of fresh problems in Corinth. He then wrote the letter we call Second Corinthians.

THE CHURCH IN CORINTH

Not all will agree with every detail of this reconstruction of Paul's life during these months, but the purpose is to highlight the extreme difficulty which Paul, the world's model church planter, endured. We should remember that the church is still a prime target of the enemy and it should be no surprise that the councils of Hell are plotting against it (Matt. 16:18). Not every sincere and gifted evangelist who follows all the advice given in a "church growth handbook" is guaranteed "success" as men count it. Nor should we be quick to count the fastest growing church as the one which God most favors.

Church Growth Leader Under Attack

Paul's second letter to the Corinthian church reveals more of his shepherd character than any in the New Testament. It is a gold mine of insights into the ministry which church growth leaders face. Paul himself is the model. In it he answers the personal attack of the Palestinian legalists who continued to harass the church in Corinth by adding Jewish ceremonial law to the message of the Gospel.

In trying to undermine Paul's authority they accused him of being double minded, a madman and an imposter, of writing deviously, being ugly, dishonest, a coward and inferior because he did not claim financial support from them. They attacked his person, contradicted his teachings and maligned his character. The major part of the letter is devoted to what true ministry really is and that, contrary to the accusations, Paul himself was eminently qualified as a minister (servant) of God.

Paul encourages the church by depicting its people as part of a triumphal procession celebrating the victory of the Gospel (2 Cor. 2:14-17). He goes on to say that in spite of his enemies he did not lose heart in church ministry because he had both the enlightenment of knowing Christ and continual inward renewal from God. So how could "temporary light affliction" be compared with the eternal weight of glory (4:1-18)? Motivated by the love of Christ he gladly continued his ministry of reconciliation (5:1-18). It is a growth principle, that even in trial and difficulty the church was directed to keep its focus on the triumph of the cross and on the coming glory.

Concern for the Churches

The final four chapters of his second letter are a vindication of Paul's ministry in which he shows clearly the differences between his legalistic detractors--"Are they ministers of Christ" (2 Cor. 11:23)?--and himself as a true minister--"I more so." He proves this by listing the hardships he had endured in his "concern for all the churches" (vv. 23-31). Like his Master he "loved the church and gave Himself up for her" (Eph. 5:25). His ministers (servants) today should do no less. The work of true shepherds who give their lives for the sheep is as great an asset to the healthy growth of New Testament churches as any other. So many churches languish for lack of such care.

The final mention about Corinth in the New Testament is in Acts 20:2,3 where we learn that Paul did get there as he had planned when he wrote Second Corinthians. He was there three months, presumably building up the church. We know that he wrote Romans from there in his continuing concern for the growth of that church. And that an offering for the poor in Jerusalem was collected from the believers in Corinth and sent with Paul. A discovered plot on his life by Jewish enemies forced him to leave secretly by road to join the couriers of similar offerings from churches in Macedonia and Asia. They were able to take the offering to Jerusalem.

THE CHURCH IN CORINTH 97

Growth Insights from Corinth

1. The tentmaking principle 84
2. Preaching for decisions 86
3. Key people and their importance 87
4. Vital help from "little people" 88
5. God's encouragement for church planters 89
6. Planting seeds and laying foundations 91
7. The danger of party spirit 91
8. Holiness is a church growth principle 93
9. The church planter under fire 95
10. The cost of the care of the churches 96

Chapter 6

THE CHURCH IN EPHESUS
The Cost of Caring
for Growing Churches

The Ephesus story is rich in both detail and insight. It spans fully forty years beginning around 51 A.D. and is documented in no less than seven New Testament books. Authors Luke, Paul and John together contribute about twenty chapters to the record of the church in Ephesus. God has given us, in the Ephesus story, the most complete model church of the Bible.

In the opening century of the Christian era Ephesus was the urban hub of Asia, the most prosperous part of the New Testament world. As a marketplace it was past its prime because its great harbor was silting up. But politically it was a world class city and its religious influence was enormous. It contained the renowned temple of the goddess Artemis, four times the size of the Parthenon in Athens and one of the "seven wonders of the ancient world."

The vision for a church in the chief city of Asia began in the mind of Paul as he prayed and planned for the expansion of the kingdom of God. While planting his first church in Pisidian Antioch near the border of Asia, Paul no doubt met travellers from that province and realized the potential for the cause of Christ and His church there. He was enough of a strategist to know that Ephesus was the key to effectively evangelizing Asia. Though he could not go immediately, the burden for Ephesus remained on his heart.

Two years later, on his second missionary journey, Paul was again in Antioch. This time, he hoped to move on west into Asia toward Ephesus. Then a strange thing happened. In Acts it is simply stated that Paul and Silas were "forbidden by the Holy Spirit to speak the word in Asia" (Acts 16:6). God stopped them from going to Ephesus at that time. Why? We can only surmise that it was not yet God's time to open the door. The result was that they evangelized the provinces of Macedonia and Achaia during the next two years. Churches were planted in Philippi, Thessalonica, Berea and Corinth. But the burden of Ephesus never left Paul.

Ready People At The Right Time

Suddenly the door opened. The church in Corinth had been planted and was growing. Paul was on his way from there to Syria and Palestine. With Priscilla and Aquila he sailed across the Aegean and came to Ephesus. He took the opportunity of a stopover to reason with the Jews in the synagogue. The Jews became interested and asked him to stay longer. But Paul was already committed to sail east and did not consent. He did, however, promise to return in a few months if God willed. He also arranged that Priscilla and Aquila stay in Ephesus, probably continuing their tentmaking business (Acts 18:19-21).

It was the presence of Priscilla and Aquila which proved to be the key to the birth of the church in Ephesus. They had been with Paul during the establishment of the church in Corinth and were, by this time, solidly grounded in the faith. Their home and tentmaking shop became the center for discipling others. They possessed the wisdom to perceive needs and then apply the Word of God.

Under-used Resource

People like Priscilla and Aquila are a valuable asset to any work for God and particularly to one newborn. As committed believers without formal religious training, they represent the most under-used resource for church planting in our contemporary world. The modern phobia for employing degreed specialists has blinded us to the potential of the marketplace Christian.

It is instructive to note Paul's patient waiting on God in reference to the timing at Ephesus. He had waited for more than two years after he was ready (Acts 16:6). Then, even when he did arrive and was invited to continue debating in the synagogue, he promised to

THE CHURCH IN EPHESUS

return only "if God wills" (18:21). His sensitivity to the guidance of the Spirit in the first instance and his willingness to "wait on the Lord" in the second demonstrate that he had learned "unless the Lord builds the house they labor in vain who build it."

PRINCIPLE: ORDINARY PEOPLE ARE A KEY FACTOR TO CHURCH GROWTH

While Paul was away from Ephesus, God continued to work through others. Priscilla and Aquila were regularly in the synagogue where Paul had opened the Christian dialogue. They were spiritually alert waiting for God to open a door. Not long after Paul left Apollos came to Ephesus. He was the brilliant Jew from Alexandria who later, as we have already noted, was such a help in Corinth. His time in Ephesus was before all that. He is described in glowing terms: "Mighty in the Scriptures... instructed in the way of the Lord...fervent in spirit... teaching accurately the things concerning Jesus" (Acts 18:24,25).

He made a powerful impression on many of the Jews in the synagogue as he opened up the Old Testament prophecies of Christ and exhorted them to prepare the "way of the Lord" which John the Baptist had proclaimed (Acts 18:25; Isa. 40:3; Matt. 3:3).

God At Work

Priscilla and Aquila were spellbound by his oratory, but they soon detected that his message of Jesus did not give the full story. Apollos had heard no more than that Jesus had been introduced by John the Baptist and had demonstrated His Messianic claims. The story infers that he did not yet know that the great events of the crucifixion, resurrection, ascension and Pentecost had all taken place.

Priscilla and Aquila acted very wisely not to embarrass Apollos, but took him aside and explained to him "the way of God more accurately" (Acts 18:26). This was a crucial moment for evangelistic impact on Ephesus. Apollos gladly accepted the truth and spoke out powerfully in Ephesus "refuting the Jews in public, demonstrating by the Scriptures that Jesus was the Christ" (vv. 26-28). The result was that people believed in Christ. No details are given about how many except that when Apollos wanted to proceed to Corinth "the brethren" wrote a letter of recommendation for him."

The wonderful working of God is evident in these beginnings at Ephesus. Without Paul's presence or personal direction, God complimented the quieter witness of Priscilla and Aquila with the attractive preaching of Apollos. The quiet couple graciously taught Apollos who was humble enough to accept the truth and preach it. Both were needed. God worked through them to provide a nucleus of believers in Jesus the Messiah (Acts 18:25-28).

Meanwhile, in another synagogue, God was preparing a second group of disciples. They too had somehow responded to the message of John the Baptist. But like Apollos they had not heard of the crucifixion, resurrection or Pentecost. Nor, does it seem, had they any contact with the "Apollos group" in Ephesus.

When Paul finally arrived in Ephesus he discovered this group and quickly perceived their incomplete faith and baptism (Acts 19:1-4). He explained to them the coming of Jesus and the whole Gospel. They immediately responded and were baptized as believers in the Name of the Lord Jesus. God confirmed their faith by giving them a Pentecost-like experience when they spoke in tongues and prophesied (vv. 4-7).[8]

In both these instances (the Apollos group and the John the Baptist group), where an inadequacy was discovered in the preaching, it became necessary to

---

[8] On the question of tongues as a sign in Acts, it may be helpful to the reader to point out that this is the fourth occasion when tongues are mentioned. Each time it was when the Gospel of the grace of God was introduced for the first time to people who had not heard it. First to the Jews in Jerusalem (Acts 2), second to the Samaritans in Samaria (Acts 8), then to the Gentiles in Caesarea (Acts 10) and finally to this group of John's disciples in Acts 19. In all four instances it was an introductory sign.

correct the situation before proceeding further. Right doctrine is of primary importance. The expediency of relationships must not allow compromise in the truth.

Thus, the beginning of this church was really the result of God's work in God's time. He burdened Paul's heart and delayed his going there until the time was right. He gifted Priscilla and Aquila to be witnesses, hosts, and discerning teachers. He brought Apollos, the preacher who stirred the city. He prepared the twelve disciples of John to receive the whole Gospel. When Paul arrived everything was ready for a remarkable evangelistic thrust which resulted in a healthy growing church.

Ephesus Bible School--Bible Study Evangelism

For the next three months Paul took the opportunity in the synagogue to speak out boldly concerning Jesus and the Kingdom of God, his usual approach. In particular he used his great powers of reason and persuasion to explain that Jesus was "the Way" (John 14:6; Acts 19:8,9). Paul himself had once been the avowed enemy of "the Way," but now he was its greatest exponent (Acts 9:2). Not everyone in the synagogue was sympathetic. Opposition began to build coming from those described as "hardened and disobedient." They publicly opposed "the Way" until Paul and the Christian disciples withdrew from the synagogue.

Paul moved his "evangelistic Bible studies" to a rented school building during the afternoons when it was not normally in use. Its owner and teacher Tyrannus, may well have become a believer and made the premises available. For two years Paul continued there reasoning every day from the Scriptures about "the Way" (Acts 19:9,10). Jews and Gentiles responded in true Christian faith. When they believed, he trained them in Christian discipleship; and the local church came into being and grew rapidly.

The reasoned approach and the solid Biblical base of their evangelism is significant. In the synagogue Paul reasoned from the Scriptures (Acts 19:8). When they moved to the school setting he continued to use the Scriptures as the textbook (v. 10). Reason and persuasion from the Word of God does not necessarily make Bible study "fun or entertaining."

In our effort to attract the unsaved, we should avoid an appeal to the emotions at the expense of the understanding. The effect of coordinated drama, music and sermon in some of our church growth efforts is no doubt pleasing. But we dare not let what is attractive to the emotions become a screen to hide aspects of the message which will bring the believer into conflict with a world system ruled by Satan. The true Gospel results in repentance from sin and a rejection of the world system.

Multiplication of Churches

A major emphasis in the "Ephesus Bible School" was on evangelistic outreach. The record states that the purpose of Paul's teaching in the school of Tyrannus was "So that all who lived in Asia heard the word of the Lord, both Jews and Greeks" (Acts 19:10 *emphasis mine*). Evangelism was not the accidental outcome of Paul's discipleship training program; it was central to the curriculum of it.

PRINCIPLE: VISION FOR GROWTH SHOULD NOT STOP AT THE LOCAL CHURCH

Ten cities of Asia surrounded Ephesus. In at least nine of them there was no existing church. Paul deliberately taught his disciples to take the Gospel to those cities, even during the growing stage of the church in Ephesus. Numerical growth in Ephesus was not the final goal. Paul encouraged the disciples to push out the boundaries of the Kingdom of God. They were never to become comfortable multiplying believers in a single church, but to be constantly thinking in terms of multiplying churches.

The insight for us is that building our local church is a legitimate goal, but only local and only short term. It is stage one in a series which extends from "Jerusalem" to "even the remotest part of the earth" (Acts 1:8). Believers with a consciousness of the

Biblical mandate will be looking beyond the "mother" church to ever increasing numbers of "daughter" churches.

The results in Ephesus were awesome. Within a few years there were churches in ten other cities of Asia, all of which are mentioned in the New Testament. The implication is that most were "daughter" churches. Grasp the impact of it as you consider these names: Smyrna, Pergamum, Thyatira, Sardis, Philadelphia, Laodicea, Colossae, Hierapolis, Miletus, Troas. Paul wrote First Corinthians from Ephesus and with obvious joy he could say "the **churches** of Asia greet you" (1 Cor. 16:19 *emphasis mine*).

The amazing results did not come without physical and emotional cost to the apostle. Paul was not just teaching a couple of hours during the afternoons. He was tentmaking during the mornings, teaching in the afternoons, instructing believers from house to house, and warning them with tears (Acts 20:20). Church planting is among the most demanding jobs in the world. Ask someone who has done it.

Another feature of the Ephesus campaign was the display of miracles or works of power. "And God was performing extraordinary miracles by the hands of Paul so that handkerchiefs or aprons were even carried from his body to the sick, and the diseases left them and the evil spirits went out" (Acts 19:11,12). Luke's account here emphasized the supernatural power of the Gospel.

The miracles were "extraordinary" in the sense that they were indirectly done through "sweat-cloths and work-aprons" rather than by the laying on of hands. They were specially accommodated to the conditions at Ephesus where magic, superstition, demonism and astrology were so evident. Paul vindicated his true apostleship by miracles here as he had at Corinth (2 Cor. 12:12). As "signs of apostleship" and as "extraordinary" we should not expect such miracles as the norm for evangelism in the 1990s.

God sometimes does do miracles today, especially in connection with evangelism in unevangelized areas where occultism is particularly strong (as it was in Ephesus). They did contribute to church growth in New Testament times. However, Scripture does not teach that people today are given spiritual gifts to perform miracles as were the apostles and prophets at the beginning of the church. Miraculous gifts were the proof of apostleship and prophethood (2 Cor. 12:12). Apostleship and prophethood were foundational, unlike the continuing gifts as evangelist, pastor/teacher etc. (Eph. 2:20; 4:11). They were directed especially at unbelieving Jews in fulfillment of Old Testament prophecies (1 Cor. 14:22; Isa. 28:11ff).

Conflict with the Occult

Some wandering Jewish exorcists arrived in Ephesus claiming occult powers and connection with the chief priests in Jerusalem. They heard Paul using the name of Jesus who had cast out demons. Then they themselves tried to use the name of Jesus as a magical device. The demon they were trying to exorcise then attacked them leaving them wounded, naked and running out of the house. They learned that they could not misuse the name of the Lord Jesus in the occult world (Acts 19:13-16).

God turned the tables on them and the incident became known all over Ephesus so that fear fell on all the Jews and Greeks. The name of the Lord Jesus, instead of being dragged into the occult world, was honored and feared in the community. Christian believers who were still dabbling in the occult were also impressed. They renounced the "hidden things of darkness" and brought their occult scrolls and held a public burning of them as a witness, with a market value of 50,000 pieces of silver. Their confession was matched by their willingness to come clean publicly (Acts 19:17-19).

It was a demonstration of the power of the Gospel and had a marked effect on Ephesus. Note it! "So the word of the Lord was growing mightily and prevailing" (Acts 19:20 *emphasis mine*). Satan's men had been publicly embarrassed. The believers had renounced their occultic practices and then openly declared the Name of the Lord Jesus. The result was that the "word of the Lord grew mightily." That's church growth--the power of the Word of God being demonstrated in changed lives and resulting in the salvation of the observers.

Two battles had passed. In the first the believers withdrew when the enemies in the synagogue spoke "evil of the Way" (Acts 19:9). In the second God stepped in to change the situation so that the occult practitioners were confounded and the Name of the Lord Jesus was magnified. But the war was not over! The councils of Hell are always scheming new attacks. Ephesus was no exception. Precisely because it was a spiritually active church, opposition was virtually guaranteed.

Conflict With The Business Community

Dateline: May 55 A.D. Paul had just written to the Corinthians praising God for the great door of the Gospel which had been opened to him (1 Cor. 16:9). In his letter to them he had mentioned that God had delivered him from wild beasts; evidently he was threatened with this kind of death in the great stadium of Ephesus. But God had stepped in (15:32). The third battle was about to begin.

It all started over shrines of the goddess Artemis (Diana) whose worship was centered in the great temple in Ephesus. The artisans who made the shrines were worried. So many people were being saved that their business was in a slump. These shrines were bought, taken to the temple to be dedicated and then used for idol worship and good luck in the homes. Even though the great annual festival of Artemis was in full swing at that very moment, the idol business was hurting. One of the leaders, Demetrius, responded by organizing a meeting of the craftsmen's guild. He blamed Paul for the slump because he preached that "the gods made with hands are no gods at all" (Acts 19:26). He spoke with concern that the goddess Artemis would fall into disrepute. Probably even more important to him was that his financial prosperity was in jeopardy (vv. 25-27).

The guild meeting became heated. Tempers rose. They spilled out into the street shouting, "Great is Artemis (Diana) of the Ephesians." Soon they were joined by hundreds, then thousands of people who made their way to the great outdoor theater of Ephesus which holds 24,500 people. Luke tells us that the majority of the people had no idea why they were shouting.

As the crowd poured into the huge theater they dragged in two of Paul's Christian friends visiting from Macedonia, Gaius and Aristarchus. They were in danger of being lynched. Paul heard what was happening and wanted to address the crowd, but was fortunately restrained by both the disciples and the provincial officials.

The confusion and shouting continued for two hours until the town clerk was able to speak, reminding the crowd that if the Roman officials, who were in the city, reported the disturbance to Rome the whole city would be in trouble. He told the people that they had legal recourse to the courts if they wished but the present meeting was illegal. He dismissed the crowd which fortunately obeyed (Acts 19:26-41).

The Gates of Hell Shall Not Prevail

The important thing for us to see is that a riot that might have killed Paul and resulted in the scattering of the infant church in Ephesus in a single day was prevented by the providence of God. Jesus' words were proved true again that "the gates (councils) of Hell shall not overpower it" (*the church*, Matt. 16:18).

The account in Acts of Paul's three years in Ephesus is by no means complete. Luke omits some events during that time which are mentioned elsewhere. We have referred to the record of Paul being thrown to wild beasts there (1 Cor. 15:32). On another occasion during his time in Ephesus Priscilla and Aquila "risked their necks" for Paul's life (Rom. 16:4). We don't know any more of that incident. In the same chapter we read of Andronicus and Junias who were Paul's "fellow-prisoners," probably in Ephesus (compare Rom. 16:7 and 2 Cor. 11:23-27). Second Corinthians was written shortly after Paul left Ephesus.

Paul left Ephesus soon after the riot and went north to Troas to join Titus. Not waiting for Titus he went on to Macedonia where Titus caught up with him bringing a letter from Corinth (2 Cor. 7:5-7). He answered them with the letter we call Second Corinthians and spent a few months encouraging the Macedonian churches and

THE CHURCH IN EPHESUS 109

visiting Illyricum (Acts 20:2; Rom. 15:19). He went on to Achaia as he had planned (Acts 19:21) spending three months in Corinth where he wrote to the Romans (2 Cor. 12:14; 1 Cor. 16:5-7; Rom. 16:23).

He intended to sail directly to Jerusalem, but a plot on his life was discovered and he took a safer route around the Aegean coastline. At Troas he joined a number of delegates from the churches of Achaia, and Macedonia who were taking a large offering for the Jewish believers in Jerusalem (Acts 20:1-6). They were anxious to get there before the Feast of Pentecost so they had not planned to stop at Ephesus. However, when their ship docked in the nearby port of Miletus, Paul took the opportunity to send for the elders of the Ephesian church who came and met him there (vv. 16,17).

Plural Leadership Promotes Healthy Growth

An important part of Paul's church growth strategy appears here. The Ephesus church was established with plural leadership (men designated as "elders," "overseers" [bishops] and "shepherds" [pastors]). All three of these terms are used in the same context of the same group of men (Acts 20:17,28). The consistent New Testament pattern is that the church should be led by men who are recognized as elders rather than by one strong decision-maker. Both the oversight of the church and the shepherd care are to come from this group as they have been gifted by God.

The New Testament pattern of church leadership provides for the New Testament pattern of church growth. Why? Because it makes use of a far greater variety of spiritual gifts than any one man possesses for wise planning and decision making. More people become involved in prayer, strategy and working. Plural leadership avoids the constant danger of a local church being built on the charisma of one man and collapsing when he goes. Plural leadership assures continuity even under persecution, as in modern churches in China and the Muslim world. Strong single leadership may result in greater numerical growth in the beginning, but will not result in the long term balanced continuity.

Counsel to Church Elders

Paul had been away from Ephesus for eighteen turbulent months. He thought that he would never have another opportunity to speak to them personally. His message to these men called elders, overseers and shepherds reveals intense concern for their spiritual well-being and their responsibility to the flock. Perhaps more than any other passage in the New Testament, this exhortation gives insight into the heart of Paul. Read it from your own Bible as a whole and feel its emotional impact (Acts 20:17-38).

This is the first of three remarkable messages to the church in Ephesus recorded in the New Testament (see also Eph. 1--6 and Rev. 2:1-7). We shall comment on the characteristics of a growing church, the character of the apostle who planted it and the responsibility of the elders who were leading it as noted here.

The Portrait of a Church Planter

The passage paints a word portrait of Paul, the model church planting evangelist. It reveals his humble, servant-like attitude which the Ephesians clearly remembered. "You yourselves know...how I was... serving with humility...with tears...with trials" (Acts 20:18,19). He verified the truth of the Christian message by demonstrating the character of Christ, especially His humility. The elders to whom Paul was speaking had all been served by Paul. So he is asking them to look at the portrait in preparation for their leadership.

Another feature of Paul's attitude which is clearly seen in the portrait is his zeal. Twice he tells us that he held back nothing from them (Acts 20:20,27). He gave himself fully to share the whole truth with the Ephesians. Night and day for three years he did not cease to admonish them with tears (v. 31). That's zeal! The discipline of hard work is one of the most necessary ingredients of church growth. Paul makes much of his example to the elders. "I showed you that by working hard in this manner you must help the weak" (v. 35).

THE CHURCH IN EPHESUS 111

Tears and Trials

Paul's humility and zeal were matched by one further aspect of his attitude which stands out in the Ephesian portrait. It is his love for souls highlighted by the words "tears and trials" (Acts 20:19). He wept for souls in the realization of their lostness and in his intense desire to win them. Evangelism is often marked by disappointments when people fail to respond to the Good News, or when they seem to respond and then fall away. Paul's Lord had wept over the people of Jerusalem when they rejected His message. The Psalmist too spoke of going out to sow the seed with tears (Psa. 126:5,6). The history of true evangelism is wet with the tears of great men like Jonathan Edwards and John Wesley. Today's evangelism, however, is known more for its slick planning than for its moist cheeks.

Tears also marked Paul's pastoral care at Ephesus. The heart of a true shepherd is a weeping heart--leading, feeding, strengthening, restoring. The bond between Paul the shepherd and the young sheep at Ephesus made him hurt when they hurt and weep when they wept. When the world with its pleasures, possessions and power made inroads into their lives he wept. When sin or death removed the most promising disciples he wept again. Like his Master at the death of Lazarus he could sympathize with their weaknesses (John 11:35; Heb. 4:15).

Paul's tears are mentioned again in our passage where he reminded them that for three years he had admonished (gently reproved) them with tears. He cared enough about their spiritual development to weep over their failures and weep as he counselled them toward restoration. The portrait of the New Testament church planter shows a weeping man.

The picture also reveals enemies in the background plotting against the apostle. Paul describes their activities resulting in "trials which came upon me through the plots of the Jews" (Acts 20:19). We have noted that conflict with the local Jews, with the occult and with the business community has plagued him in Ephesus. Now he is plagued by the plots of the outside Jewish teachers. It had happened before in Antioch, Galatia, Thessalonica, Berea and Corinth. Paul's severest trials came from his fellow Jews. Some of the most damaging adversaries of evangelism for us too are groups with names like "christian" and "church" attached to them.

Ministry Model for Growing Churches

Paul's message to the elders in Acts 20 reveals a superb model of how he ministered to a young and growing church. He taught them thoroughly, both publicly and privately from house to house (Acts 20:20). A good case can be established from this passage for a two-pronged thrust of teaching. First publicly to a general audience and then more privately in the homes of the committed believers. A modern parallel would be the expository teaching from the pulpit aided by the intimacy of the home Bible study group. Jesus used the same tactic when he taught the multitudes with parables and then later explained them more clearly and intimately to the disciples (Matt. 13:24-30,36-43).

The content of Paul's teaching to the young believers was more than a message designed to get his hearers to come back to "church" again. Of interest is the specific statement that he did not shrink from declaring anything that was profitable (Acts 20:20). Evidently he was tempted to soften the implications of the whole truth so as not to arouse the wrath of the heathen or to compromise with the Jewish legalists. Paul would not "draw back" so that the whole purpose of God was expounded to them (vv. 20,27).

The spiritual diet designed for optimum growth might surprise us. It included repentance toward God because of sin, and faith in the Lord Jesus Christ (Acts 20:21). He also taught the grace of God as the basis for the building of holy Christian character (v. 24). Faith and grace were balanced with a right perspective on the Kingdom and submission to the King (v. 25). The second coming of Christ and His future reign directly influenced the attitudes and lifestyles of contemporary disciples. The point is that the young church was given the strong meat of the Word as a solid Biblical diet on which to grow. It was the living God and the Word of His grace which was able to build them up (v. 32).

Wolf Alert

For the Ephesians, as for us today, it was of utmost importance to be firmly grounded in the Truth. False teachers whom Paul calls "savage wolves" were soon to attack the flock of God. The elders would have to be on the alert for them and constantly be guarding the flock (Acts 20:28,29). The "wolves" would appear from two directions: some from outside the church and some from among the elders themselves (vv. 29,30). They would be identified as men speaking perverse (corrupted or twisted) things and drawing away the disciples after themselves (v. 30).

The counterparts in our day are those caught up in the different "isms" who develop followings and split churches. Their error ranges from supplementing the requirements of the Gospel to removing its vital essentials. Emissaries arrive at our doors with persuasive talk and attractive literature, full of sweetened lies. Television pictures and sounds invade our family rooms. The church's shepherds must be constantly alert and prepare the sheep to withstand the attack. The warning ministry of the shepherds must not be silenced under the false idea that "Christian love" embraces everything that calls itself Christian.

The Ephesian elders are specially warned to be on guard for a wolf among their own number where the most insidious danger might lie in wait. The danger was that they attract disciples to themselves rather than to the Lord Jesus; building a personal following which one day may split the church. How often this has happened.

Note carefully that the reason for the exhortation to the shepherds and the warning about the danger of wolves is that the church is so precious to God. Between these two exhortations is the statement that the flock has been purchased with His own blood (Acts 20:28-31). The Great Shepherd paid the infinite price for the sheep which make up the church. The sheep are His. He purchased them. The elders therefore are charged with the responsibility of caring for and protecting someone else's possession. And it's the most costly possession in the universe. Awesome!

Paul's final comment to the Ephesian elders was to remind them that he had worked hard with his hands in secular employment to meet financial needs, his own and those of his fellow workers (Acts 20:34). He instructs the elders to work hard so that they could help the weak, to learn the joy of giving as the Lord Jesus had taught (v. 35). Perhaps more attention ought to be paid to this passage by church leaders in our society.

Paul's exhortation to the elders ended with a touching scene of Christian love as they embraced him with tears thinking that they would never see him again on earth.[9]

A Gift for Jerusalem

On leaving Ephesus his immediate objective was to visit Jerusalem in time for Pentecost with the gifts from the Gentile churches to the Jewish Christians there. The church of Ephesus had joined with many others in this collective offering. Ephesus sent two Gentile couriers with their contribution, Trophimus and Tychichus (Acts 20:4). Paul hoped that both the gift itself and the Gentile background of the couriers would help bridge the growing rift between Jewish legalists and Gentile believers (Rom. 15:31). As it turned out, Trophimus was embroiled in a misunderstanding which sparked a mob scene and resulted in Paul's imprisonment (Acts 21--23).

From Jerusalem Paul was transferred to a prison in Caesarea where he was kept two years. Eventually he appealed his case to Caesar Nero in Rome and was taken there (Acts 27--28). Several years had elapsed before He was again in direct contact with the church in Ephesus.

God Had His People

The growth of a local church is not dependent only on the talents of one good leader, but rests on the combined efforts of many talented people.

---

[9]In all probability Paul did visit Ephesus again four or five years later between his two Roman imprisonments about 63 A.D.

But God had not left the church an orphan. He may remove his workers, but He carries on His work. God continued His work using people He had placed there. Priscilla and Aquila were back after a period in Rome (Rom. 16:3; 2 Tim. 4:19). We have already noted this talented couple. Onesiphorus and his family were there. He was well known for his Christian boldness and for the "services he rendered at Ephesus." He was a caring man for he went to Rome and "often refreshed" the apostle in prison (2 Tim. 1:16-18).

Timothy is a valuable addition to that list. He had been with Paul in the early days of the church of Ephesus (1 Cor. 4:17; Acts 19:22). He was there when Paul gave his farewell address to the elders (Acts 20:4). He probably went on to Jerusalem with Paul, but returned to teach the faith and to combat the heretics after Paul was imprisoned. When he heard Paul was in Rome he went to help. Paul said "I have no one like him" (Phil 1:1; 2:20-22; Col. 1:1). Later he returned to Ephesus for the fourth time, where he received two pastoral letters from Paul who was again in prison (1 and 2 Timothy). Timothy's name belongs with the church growth story in Ephesus.

Letter to a Growing Church

In the spring of 61 A.D. Paul the prisoner arrived in Rome after a long and eventful voyage, accompanied by Luke and Aristarchus (Acts 27--28). While kept under minimum security, he was able to contact leaders of the Jewish community (Acts 28:17-29), as well as the Christians in the churches to whom he had already written the letter we call the Epistle to the Romans (vv. 30-31). During the two years of his first imprisonment in Rome he wrote four letters, one of which was directed to the church in Ephesus.

His letter to the Christians in Ephesus emphasizes the great truths of Christ and His church. It is theological truth at its best. Sometimes we forget, however, that these truths were not written to seminary students, but to a growing local church for the sake of its life and health. Doctrine is never simply academic, but intensely practical and necessary if the church is to survive. Nor is doctrine for the leaders only, a mistaken notion that is all too common today. Consider the growth implications of the letter.

Their Inheritance in Christ

Three sections clearly emphasize the major themes in the letter. In the first section growth is seen as a characteristic of the very nature of the church as the living body of Christ (Eph. 1--3). He rose from the dead to become its living Head. Having risen with Christ the church is heir to all the riches of His grace in the heavenly places. Paul prays that they may fully comprehend the glory of their inheritance in Christ and know the indwelling power of His resurrection (Eph. 1:11-23). He goes on to explain that there is only one body (the church) brought into being by the finished work of Christ (ch. 2). Paul prays a second time for them, this time that they might be strengthened to fully understand the magnitude of Christ's love which has lifted her to her place in the heavenly places (3:16-19). The first three chapters emphasize that the church is seen in the context of its heavenly position. From this position we appropriate the "power that works within us" from "Him who is able to do exceeding abundantly beyond all that we ask or think" (3:20-21). It is important for believers to grasp this intensely practical truth.

Their Behavior in a Corrupt World

The church in Ephesus was instructed to behave in a way consistent with the calling of God to their inheritance (Eph. 4--5). As the physical body grows and develops to maturity, so the church as a spiritual body is to come to maturity, to the stature of the fullness of Christ. For "the building up of the body" (i.e church growth) the risen Christ gave gifts to the church (Eph. 4:8-12). As these gifts are used, the church grows. An emphasis in this chapter is that the "proper working of each individual part causes the growth of the body for the building up of itself in love (v. 16). Every part of the body has an important function in its growth.

Their Conflict With a Wily Enemy

Paul urges the Ephesian church to be strong in the Lord because she is in conflict with a powerful enemy who is scheming to destroy her. The cosmic battle which has been going on since Satan was cast out of heaven is being fought in the arena of the heavenly sphere where the church is. Paul reminds the Ephesians of the cosmic nature of the battle, "against the spiritual forces of wickedness in the heavenly places," and then urges them to put on the whole armor of God as they stand against the schemes of the devil (Eph. 6:10-18).

To Timothy, Guard the Gospel

After Paul wrote the letter to the believers at Ephesus from prison in Rome we cannot state his movements precisely. Modern scholars believe that he was released from prison after about two years and spent some time with Timothy going to Spain and possibly to Cyprus and the west coast of Asia which included Ephesus. He evidently left Timothy there and went on north to Macedonia where he probably wrote the first letter to Timothy. He then was soon re-arrested and taken back to prison in Rome. Within a relatively short period he was executed. During this second Roman imprisonment he wrote a second letter to Timothy. These two letters to Timothy in Ephesus give us some insight into conditions in the church there.

Timothy's ministry in the church was not as a settled pastor. He was "urged" by Paul to "remain" there to "instruct certain men not to teach strange doctrines." These men wanted to be "teachers of the Law" but Paul asserts that they did "not understand" it (1 Tim. 1:3-7). The danger of "wolves" of whom Paul had warned them, was becoming a reality. In the first chapter Paul reminds Timothy that the "glorious gospel" had been entrusted to him (v. 11) and that he was passing on that trust to Timothy (v. 18) who was to "fight the good fight" and "keep the faith" (vv. 18,19).

The letter goes on to deal with instructions for men and women in the assembly (1 Tim. 2), qualifications for leadership (ch. 3) and the coming conditions of the "last times" when true godliness is the answer to departure from the faith (ch. 4). He gives instructions about the care of widows (ch. 5) and then repeats his charge in the last chapter. "Fight the good fight...keep the commandment without stain...O Timothy, guard what has been entrusted to you (6:12,14,20).

Paul's second letter to Timothy in Ephesus written during his second imprisonment in Rome is even more urgent. In it he appeals to the younger man to keep the truth, just as it had been taught to him, and to pass it on untainted to faithful men even at the cost of suffering (2 Tim. 1--2). The third chapter reminds Timothy of the coming difficult times when men of depraved minds would oppose the Truth. His resource was to be in the Scriptures which are inspired by God. In the final chapter the charge is solemnly repeated to Timothy as Paul indicates that his own life and ministry are soon to be poured out as a drink offering (ch. 4). Probably within a month Paul was beheaded by Caesar Nero on the Ostian Way outside Rome in the year 65 or 66 A.D.

The Biblical record of the Ephesus church growth story includes one last brief chapter. Thirty more years had elapsed when the Apostle John included it in his writings from the Isle of Patmos in about 95 A.D. Most scholars believe that John spent his later years in Ephesus from where he was exiled to the nearby prison island because of "the word of God and the testimony of Jesus" (Rev. 1:9). There God gave him a revelation instructing him to write letters to seven churches in Asia (vv. 10-11). The first letter was to Ephesus which reveals some interesting insights about the state of the church at that time (2:1-7).

The Church Where Love Died

On four counts the Lord congratulated the church. They had steadfastly persevered in their work for the Lord. They had refused to tolerate evil men concerning whom Paul had warned them. They had endured suffering for the Name of the Lord Jesus. And finally they had not grown weary through it all (Rev. 2:2,3).

But there was one fatal flaw. They had failed to follow Paul's instruction to them to "walk in love just as Christ also loved" (Eph. 5:2). There had been nineteen other references to love in Paul's letter to them. But now the Lord asserts, "You have left your first love" (Rev. 2:4). Their heart devotion to the Lord Jesus had grown cold. They had left (literally forsaken) Him. A "second" love had taken the place of their "first" love for Him.

For any church this is the beginning of the end, unless its people repent and recapture their first love for the Lord. There is no indication in Scripture about how the Ephesians responded. The Biblical record falls silent. We do know that the church continued for several centuries before the lampstand was removed completely. Today Islam rules there uncontested. The final lesson from Ephesus of its lost love is perhaps the most solemn of all. May we take careful heed.

GROWTH INSIGHTS FROM EPHESUS

1. Sensitivity to God's timing 100
2. Recognizing God at work without human planning 101
3. Variety of gift in planting ministry 102
4. Evangelism through Bible studies 103
5. A church for every city 104
6. Conflict with the occult 106
7. Conflict with the business community 107
8. Counsel to the church elders 110
9. Portrait of a church planter 110
10. Tears and trials 111
11. Teaching the whole truth 112
12. Wolf alert, enemies lurking 113
13. Leaders as working models 114
14. Others God used in church growth 115
15. Combined effort of talented people 115
16. Church growth through correspondence 115
17. Guarding the Gospel 117
18. Church growth in mortal danger 118

Chapter 7

CONCLUSION
Additional Data, Executive Summary

To complete the data base for church growth principles in the New Testament would require mention of at least 21 additional churches, not counting those in Judea.[10] The available data concerning each is significantly less than for those we have considered. However, the growth principles revealed in them are identical. For readers who may want to examine all the data we list references for the individual churches as well as groups of churches mentioned in provincial areas. A study of these would be most rewarding. Colosse and Berea have both been mentioned briefly in the text, but are listed again here.

Paul had a part in the beginnings of some of them like Berea and Cenchrea. He participated in the later growth of others like Colosse, Rome, Hierapolis, Laodicea and Miletus. Aquila and Priscilla, Timothy, Silas, Barnabas, Phoebe, Luke, Epaphras and Titus are also linked to the growth of some of these. All of them fall within Paul's sphere of influence. Philip probably founded the church in Caesarea. Peter had wide associations with believers throughout Pontus, Galatia, Cappadocia, Asia and Bithynia though no specific churches are mentioned, he does specially mention the church in Babylon (1 Pet. 5:13).

John the Apostle lived in Ephesus for many years until near the end of the first century. During an imprisonment on the nearby island of Patmos he recorded

---

[10] We have purposefully omitted Jerusalem and other Judean churches because of their strong ties to Judaism and temple worship before the destruction of Jerusalem in 70 A.D. This fact means that they were not typical New Testament churches, and therefore not models for today.

messages from the Lord to seven of the churches in the province of Asia (Rev. 2--3).

Churches in Cities of the New Testament
(Those not previously listed)

Colosse	Col. 1--4; Philemon 1:1-25
Rome	Rom. 1:7-15; 15:14-33; Acts 18:2; 19:21; 23:11; 25:11-12; 28:13-31
Caesarea	Acts 8:40; 9:30; 10:1--11:18; 18:22; 21:8-15; 24:23
Samaria	Acts 8:1-25; 9:31; 15:3
Lydda	Acts 9:32-35,38
Berea	Acts 17:10-15
Cenchrea	Acts 18:18; Rom. 16:1,2
Troas	Acts 20:6
Miletus	Acts 20:15-28; 2 Tim. 4:20
Tyre	Acts 21:4
Puteoli	Acts 28:13-14
Nicopolis	Tit. 3:12
Heirapolis	Col. 4:13
Babylon	1 Pet. 5:13
Smyrna	Rev. 2:8-11
Pergamum	Rev. 2:12-17
Thyatira	Rev. 2:18-29
Sardis	Rev. 3:1-6
Philadelphia	Rev. 3:7-13
Laodicea	Rev. 3:14-22

Groups of Churches in Provinces of the N.T. World

Phrygia	Acts 2:10; 16:6; 18:23
Phoenicia	Acts 11:19; 15:3; 21:2-7; 27:3
Dalmatia	Rom. 15:19; 2 Tim. 4:10
Cyprus	Acts 11:19-20; 13:4-12; 15:39; 21:16
Crete	Acts 2:11; 27:7-13; Tit. 1:5
Cilitia	Acts 15:23,41; 27:5; Gal. 1:21
Galatia	Acts 13:14--14:27; 15:36--16:6; 18:23; 20:4; 1 Cor. 16:1-4; 2 Cor. 12:1-5; Gal. 1--6; 2 Tim. 4:10; 1 Pet. 1:1

CONCLUSION 123

Achaia	Acts 18:12,27; 19:21; 20:2; Rom. 15:26; 1 Cor. 15:16; 2 Cor. 1:1; 9:1-4; 11:10; 1 Thess. 1:7,8
Asia	Acts 16:6; 18:19-28; 19:1-41; 20:4,15-38; 1 Cor. 16:19; 2 Cor. 1:3-11; 2 Tim. 1:15
Macedonia	Acts 16:9--17:14; 19:21-22; 20:1-6; 27:2 Rom. 15:25-27; 1 Cor. 16:5; 2 Cor. 1:16; 2:13; 7:5-16; 8:1-5; 9:2-4; 11:9; Phil. 4:15-19; 1 Thess. 1:7,8; 4:10; 2 Thess. 1:3; 1 Tim. 1:3
Pontus	1 Pet. 1:1
Cappadocia	Acts 2:9; 1 Pet. 1:1
Bithynia	Acts 16:7; 1 Pet. 1:1

The principles pointed out from the data in the chapters of this book are helpful to us in our local churches only as we put them into practice. We are persuaded that God's work, done according to the principles in His Word, will prosper. It is up to us how we apply them.

It ought to be obvious that the growth of a spiritual organism (the church) requires more than the principles of sociology used by secular organizations; more than the charisma of a great leader; more than crowds of people; more than a first class facility in a good neighborhood. Biblical church growth requires people who love the Lord Jesus Christ and have committed their lives to obey Him. They are convinced that the Word of God is their guide and that its principles are sure.

Melvin Hodges sums it up well:

> We can study methods of church growth and write books about indigenous church principles, all of which is well and good: but we will never have anything like New Testament churches and New Testament growth until we get something like New Testament men with New Testament experience. I do not know how this affects you, but it challenges me to the depths of my being.

124 BIBLICAL PRINCIPLES OF CHURCH GROWTH

God's methods are men and we are the men. [11]

Paul is the greatest exponent of church growth in the Bible. His applied principles of church growth follow three clear stages seen in all six of the churches considered in this book. First there was the **evangelistic stage** when the emphasis was on the presentation of the Gospel, using relational bridges and adapting this to culturally acceptable methods.

Second, there was the **teaching stage** added to the continuing evangelistic thrust. Believers were trained to be disciples in every sense of the word. They became people of the Word: praying people, loving people, serving people, worshipping people, witnessing people, and fellowshipping people. All this happened not by accident but by careful and costly training.

Finally, there was an **indigenous growth stage**. The church continued to grow in both quality and numbers without the parental care of the founder. It had become self-governing, self-supporting and self-propagating based on the principles which have been left to us in the New Testament models. Paul, and others, could leave a healthy growing church not dependent on any one leader. That's pauline church growth!

Michael Borodin was sent to China in 1923 by Lenin as a special advisor from the Communist Party in Russia. His job was to help reorganize the Kuomintang into a highly disciplined central party. His most promising students were Sun Yat Sen, Chiang Kai-shek and a young man from Vietnam named Ho Chi-minh.

Borodin was interviewed by an American correspondent concerning his purpose to take over China for the Communist movement. The correspondent finally said, "You are too few, you'll never do it."

"O yes we will," came the cool reply. "You forget, young man, that I am not here for my health, comfort or personal success. I am totally dedicated to the cause of the Communist movement."

---

[11]*Church Growth and Church Mission*. Grand Rapids: Eerdmans, n.d.

CONCLUSION 125

After a long silence, Borodin began to murmur, half to himself, "You know," he mused, "I used to read the New Testament. It is the most wonderful story ever told. That man Paul, he was a real revolutionary. I take my hat off to him."

Suddenly Borodin whirled around and shook his fist in the face of the correspondent. "But where do you find him today," he shouted. "Answer me that, where do you find him today?"